29p

GW00361226

The Punch Book of Health

_____

Edited by
William Davis

CORONET BOOKS
Hodder and Stoughton

First published in Great Britain 1975 by
Punch Publications Limited

Coronet Edition 1976

———————————————————

Printed and bound in Great Britain for Coronet Books,
Hodder and Stoughton, London, by The Leagrave Press

ISBN 0 340 20999 2

The Punch Book of
HEALTH

edited by William Davis

THE PREVAILING EPIDEMIC.

"Ah! You may laugh, my boy; but it's no joke being funny with the influenza"

CONTENTS

Give Me Some More of the Brown Medicine   *Basil Boothroyd*   9

Health-Hydro   *Graham*   12

A Land Flowing with Yoghurt and Carrot Juice   *Alan Whicker*   14

Songs of Food Production   19

The Health Food Fad   *Heath*   20

Enough is Enough   *Clive Barnes*   22

Golf Psychiatrist   *David Langdon*   26

How to Keep Healthy in Fog   29

The New Hygiene   31

How Sick Are The Doctors?   *Richard Gordon*   35

Ungeneral Practices   *William Hewison*   39

On A Clear Day You Can Saw For Ever   *Miles Kington*   41

Meanwhile, Back at the Ranch-Style Split-Level Surgery
    Arnold Roth   47

Blood Money   *Keith Waterhouse*   48

Bupaman   *Graham*   52

Scalpel, Forceps, Green Stamps . . .   *Alan Coren*   54

What Price the Hippocratic Oath?   *Christine Pickard*   58

The Iatrogenic Disease   *Olga Franklin*   61

A Little of What You Fancy   *Brian Inglis*   64

Patients' Association   *Larry*   70

Visitors to Britain!   73

Hospital Splendide   *Heath*   76

Love Letters to a Doctor   *Miles Kington*   78

Doctor *v.* Patient   *David Langdon*   82

Doctor on the Screen   84

A Patient's Casebook   *David Stone*   86

Food for Fears   *R. G. G. Price*   88

A Vision in Harley Street   *E. S. Turner*   91

Doctors that overcharge   *Arnold Roth*   92

In Sickness and in Health   *Alan Coren*   94

Get Well Cards   98

Scalpel, swab, scissors, lights . . . phrase-book   *J. E. Hinder*   100

A Touch of 'Flu   *Graham*   102

Doctor Patel's Diary   *Miles Kington*   104

Licensed Hospital   *Larry*   108

The Cure   *ffolkes*   110

The Avoidance of Stress and Worry   111

The Medical Book   *H. M. Bateman*   113

My Medical Article   *Basil Boothroyd*   114

The Mystery of Medicine   118

An Ideal Medical Board   120

Hay Fever   125

Better than Expected   *Richard Gordon*   129

A Domestic Tragedy   *A. T. Smith*   135

O Death Where is Thy Sting-a-ling-a-ling   *Vincent Mulchrone*   138

When You've Got to Go   *Heath*   142

Introduction

IF ever you feel depressed about inflation, trade gaps, strikes and all the other modern ills (and how can one possibly avoid it?) consider this. Six centuries ago the Black Death wiped out much of Britain's population and even a hundred years ago medicine was, by today's standards, fairly primitive. Of all the advances in this remarkable century the progress made in this particular area is, for me, the most reassuring of all. It is easy to take good health for granted; most of us do. But imagine the terrors surgery held before anaesthetics or the helplessness so many people felt before the discovery of drugs like penicillin. When I started to select material for this book (a natural successor I suppose, to earlier volumes like the *Punch Guide to Good Living*) I was very much struck by some of the cartoons we published on the subject of health (or, if you prefer, sickness) more than a century ago. I have included them in the hope that they will help to put things into perspective. I have added more recent features on health farms, health foods and drugs because they are very much part of the current scene. And there are a few words (and cartoons) on a subject which an astonishing number of people insist should be regarded as taboo: death. But my chief aim, as always, has been to provide a mixture of sharp comment and cheer.

A bore is someone who, when you ask him how he is, tells you. We talk about health in the same way as we do about the weather: it's routine dialogue, like the patter in an end-of-the-pier show or a current affairs programme like *Panorama*. Personally I have always agreed with Bulwer-Lytton:

> Refuse to be ill. Never tell people you are ill: never own it to yourself. Illness is one of those things which a man should resist on principle at the outset.

But there obviously are people who enjoy ill health, and even more who have an infinite capacity for faking pains. They just can't leave being well enough alone. Their favourite bedside reading is the *Dictionary of Symptoms* and the peak of achievement is to have an operation—after which, inevitably, scars are shown off like campaign medals. One can, of course, see the appeal: the sick man (or the man who imagines himself to be sick) is the object of much sympathy and attention. It brings drama to a life somewhat humdrum between checking one week's pools coupon and the next. But I, for one, prefer the company of people who accept that the question "how are you?" requires no answer other than "fine, thanks".

Our chief medical expert at *Punch* is the delightfully irreverent Richard Gordon and I was interested to read, as I am sure you will be, his article on sick doctors. "Sickness being such a social disaster," he says, "most doctors simply refuse to contemplate it, as the detective never expects to be burgled nor the vicar to go to hell. When it inevitably comes, the illness is taken as an affront, an insult, a stroke of treachery. And death is quite outrageous—a nasty piece of double-dealing by a long-familiar and respected accomplice."

Richard has four basic rules of health: don't smoke cigarettes, keep your weight down, take regular exercise, and look both ways before stepping off the pavement. I dare say there are fellow professionals who will quarrel with his formula: in medicine, as in economics, there is clearly room for more than one opinion. But it is one of the many bits of free advice volunteered in this book and, who knows, it may work.

For doctors, I suppose, the best service we can provide is to tell the story of a GP who, after years of party-going, finally hit on a way of getting rid of people who spoil his evenings by asking him for medical advice. "When someone begins telling me his ailments," he says, "I stop him with one word: "Undress!"".

William Davis

Give Me Some More
Of The Brown Medicine

by BASIL BOOTHROYD

YOU can't say they don't look after us. This latest move, to keep flat-dwellers fit and happy, is a real paternalistic break-through, if you ask me. "Flat neurosis" is the great danger, according to one of the doctors who says we should all have a medical examination before living in mid-air, and the symptoms certainly sound pretty nasty: headaches we might get, fits of temper, disturbed sleep and weeping attacks. Also lack of appetite and loss of weight, which a less thorough man might have bracketed together.

As soon as I read about this I was round there.

"I've come for my free check-up," I said, showing him my cutting from the Whitsun bank holiday *Times*, which was so stuck for news that day that even its business supplement was down to four pages.

"Who said anything about free?" he said, grabbing it. "These damned newspapers——" But when he saw that I'd just slipped the free in as a calm assumption he cooled off a bit. "So you think you've got flat neurosis," he said.

Something very like it, I told him.

"Headaches?" he said.

"Sometimes."

"Good. I see, I mean." I've never invented a disease myself, but I suppose if you do it's gratifying when someone comes along who's got it.

"How's the appetite?"

"I lose it sometimes."

"Weight?"

"If I lose the appetite I lose the weight. That's what I find."

"Ah," said the doctor, making a note. "What about fits of temper?"

"I have those."

"And your sleep is disturbed?"

"Very. It's the owls."

"The what? How many floors up are you?"

"One."

"Now, just a minute," he said.

"But not during the daytime. I'm not up a floor at all until I go upstairs at night. To have my sleep disturbed by the jets from Gatwick. And car doors slamming. And the plumbing. The radia-tors——"

"I thought you said owls? We're going to get——"

"And owls."

"We're going to get in a mess here," he said, "if we don't come to some sort of understanding." He pinched the bridge of his nose and squeezed his eyes shut, like a man with a headache. "Let's start again. You think you've got flat neurosis."

"A form of it."

"What form?"

"House neurosis," I said.

"You mean you don't live in a flat?"

"No. A house."

"But you're thinking of moving to a flat?"

"Not really."

"What are you wasting my time for, then?" He waved the cutting "You can see what it says here. Flat neurosis. What's that got to do with people living in houses?"

"I should have thought plenty," I said. "If the symptoms are the same. I realise, of course, that you may take a different view, professionally. If it's against your ethics, or anything, to treat a patient who's caught his disease in a house, when he should by rights have caught it in a flat, let's say no more about it, and I'll just ask you to recommend a good house neurosis doctor and I'll push off. But taking the lay view, I should have thought it didn't matter where you picked up a thing like this, as long as you've got it. And isn't it of some interest to you, in any case, to find that people can get flat neurosis in houses? It widens your whole field of specialisation, if that's not a contradiction in——"

"Shut up," he said.

"——terms," I said.

"All right," he said. "All right." He mastered something that might well have been a weeping attack.

"I'll let you off the owls," I said. "I realise that flat doctors, with patients twenty floors up, don't have to prescribe for owls much. Not even in Richmond Park. But when it comes to the plumbing——"

"I'm not a——"

"I know that. But if you're examining a man who wants to live in a flat but thinks he'll be kept awake by radiators suddenly going blang-blang in the small hours, and rushing a lot of loose water through their systems even though the central heating's been off since midnight, what would your recommendation be?"

"But these are your own radiators?"

"Very nearly. The bank——"

"Just so. That's where you fail to come within my purview."

"I do?"

"Flat-dwelling neuroses stem largely from people in the other flats."

"And *their* radiators, eh?"

"Exactly. Over which they have no control."

"I've no control over mine."

"You mentioned headaches. What sort of headaches?"

"All sorts. Money headaches. Gardening headaches. Doors-jamming-when-it-rains headaches. Peeling-wallpaper-in-the-spare-room headaches. In fact, a whole lot of headaches you don't get in flats, where it's all done by the landlord or you haul him up in front of a tri——"

"Money headaches they can still have."

*"Only you could get writer's cramp through
signing on at the labour exchange!"*

"You can prescribe for those?"

"Look," said the doctor. "I don't think we're getting anywhere with this. There's nothing here"—he handed back the cutting—"that says I'm going to *cure* flat neurosis, is there? Just diagnose, right?"

"That's what I thought," I said. "But when a patient comes to you and you decide he's got it, you're going to advise him, surely?"

"Of course. Advise him not to go and live in a flat."

"Suppose he's living in one already?"

"Advise him to get out of it."

"Into what?"

"I——"

"Because if he isn't in a flat, with flat neurosis, he's got to be in a house, with house neurosis."

"Get out," said the doctor.

"I suppose you could advise a tent, with tent neurosis, or a cave, with——"

"Three guineas. Pay the receptionist."

"The fact is," I said, "you can get your neurosis anywhere."

"I've asked you to leave." He hit his little brass bell, too hard, and wrung his hand.

"Everywhere," I said. "The rich man in his castle, the——"

"Go," he said, rising white-lipped and bending a letter-opener into a hoop.

"Right," I said. "But can you advise anywhere to go, in the times we live in, where headaches, disturbed sleep, weeping attacks, loss of——?"

He threw his Gray's *Anatomy*, and I had to duck and run without asking about fits of temper.

Health-Hydro

GRAHAM sweats it out

"Fanny Cradock!"

"The goldfish!"

"Why's he got more carrot juice than I have?"

12

"Here comes Oliver Twist!"

"Another success, Robson—came in
obese, going out fat."

13

A Land Flowing with Yoghurt and Carrot Juice

ALAN WHICKER down on the health farm

ANYONE can be beautiful and loved: it's just a question of applying something, take a course, buying a pot, denying yourself—or being operated on, slightly. So say the Archpriests of the religion of beauty, which women spend £100,000,000 a year to practise. To keep up in the Face Race, the average woman in her lifetime also spends four years fourteen weeks and six days in front of her mirror, making-up. It certainly feels that way when you're waiting downstairs.

Men—apart from the fringe fringe—seem unprepared to do much, though still pay-out a crafty £8,000,000 a year; would you believe—*guy*lashes!

By the end of this decade Americans will have spent £4,000,000,000 to make themselves a little lovelier each day—or maybe, to buy a little hope. In view of all this I went to Texas (of course) to observe a species in The Greenhouse, that ultimate purpose-built fat farm which cost a million pounds to contrive and is quite improbable. It stands, a perfumed palace outside Arlington, bathed in the soft glow of money and dedicated to the sale of dreams, the expectation of beauty.

Women of a certain age (and some younger) queue to pay from £50 to £110 a *day* for rejuvenation. Some stay months. The ageing and wrinkled, the plump and bored surrender dollars and dignity in exchange for solace and repair, for the dream of growing younger, fairer, sexier . . . while outside in the harsh sunlight, gardeners symbolically dye dry Texas grass green.

In Britain where we at least let grass decide its own colour, narcissism is also in—observe the march of fully booked Health Farms. Prices may be less extreme but you can still lose, along with avoirdupois, some ninety guineas a week.

A Health Farm means paying a lot of money *not* to do something. At the end of the week you get a breathtaking bill for what you could easily have done at home for nothing if you had the strength of character, which you haven't—so pay up and look small.

I was introduced to an early version fifteen years ago, surrendering to its rigours for a radio programme, and later for *Panorama*. Afterwards a number of patients, affronted by evident truths and being filmed Before instead of After, complained to the BBC. They did not notice I was hooked on the good sense of it all.

Such instant affront is one of the problems of television: nobody wants an accurate image of anything near to home; the preferred picture is blurred, gently distorted, romanticised, approving.

I filmed a *Whicker's World* programme on a most enjoyable cruise. Afterwards the shipping line spokesman said ruefully: "It was an honest programme, all right. The only trouble was, it was *too* honest." That's the way it goes, tellywise.

At this Surrey health hydro a few were ill but the majority were, quite reasonably, carboholics resisting the temptation, alcoholics drying-out, executives escaping the telephone: "My Chairman goes to the South of France and puts on a stone. I come here and lose one. He feels guilty; I feel great."

Health farms vary from earnest nature cure centres catering for those with little faith in orthodox medicine to stately but antiseptic Victorian mansions where society matrons hold back the years and Show Biz straightens its elbow and resists the sweet smell of excess.

If you are *not* sick there's no doubt one of the cheerier hydros, full of jolly folk expensively repenting excess, is more agreeable than those chintzy halls where arthritic old ladies knit by the fireside, each a silent reproach to the healthy but weak-willed who just want to lose a few pounds, regardless.

Voluntarily incarcerated in one of the serious establishments, I was watching a television play one night amid an enthralled group in dressing gowns; just getting to the exciting bit when a young man in the statutory white Kildare-coat strode in and switched the set off in mid-sentence. I leapt up in outrage.

"Ten o'clock," he said, reproachfully. "Time for bed." I was about to dash him to the ground when it came to me this was what we were paying for: a return to the secure days of Nanny-knows-best.

Once you've accepted such discipline there's a certain relief in surrendering to white-coated father-figures who know what's good for you, in having your days planned down to the last orange juice. There's the grin-and-bear-it Dunkirk spirit of the carrot cocktail bar where you swop losses; the lazy pastoral pleasures of a country estate; the satisfaction of growing, if not a little lovelier, at least a little *smaller* each day.

I remember another Correspondent in Ismailia during the riotous days when the Egyptians put a match to Shepherds, the late Bernard Wicksteed who wrote Tubby Hubby columns for the *Daily Express;* when he left his first health farm, he told me, he was "walking a foot off the ground." There surely is new delight in old suits that not only fasten without strain, but hang loose.

We are today in the middle of an expansionist trend, with 10 million men and 12 million women overweight. Insurance companies say a man of 45 who is 25 pounds above his proper weight lowers his expectation of life by 20%. Put another way, he'll die at 60 when he might have reached 80 . . . We spend £25 million a year on slimming foods which taste like crushed cardboard, lotions, massage equipment, pills; but you lose it best by practising one simple exercise, performed sitting down—and don't think it's easy. You shake the head from side to side when offered a fattening plateful.

A sensible girl I took out in New York refused her apple pie à la mode with the telling comment: "A moment on the lips, a lifetime on the hips."

Americans, needless to say, have the ultimate diet: the Zero-Calorie, which means you just don't eat. As you might expect, it works.

Elaine Johnson, a 35-year-old housewife, was almost 20 stone and so fat she couldn't cross her legs, or sit without breaking the chair. She started the diet after getting wedged in a cafeteria doorway, a significant time to face facts. In four months she lost eight stone. At the same California hospital Bert Goldner weighed 425 lbs.—almost 4 cwt.—and was so spherical he couldn't sit or lie without fainting from lack of oxygen. He had to sleep standing up or kneeling. During a nap he once toppled over and broke his leg.

You see how helpful it is—*reading* about diets. I feel thinner already.

The form at a fat farm is a Sunday arrival with a pseudo-medical test that evening: blood pressure, heart beats, weight and the old

HEATH

16

Army how-do-you-feel routine. The usual treatment is a complete fast, by which they mean three oranges a day. Should you be determined to surrender the whole hog, three glasses of hot water each day, with a slice of lemon to take the taste away.

Mornings are filled with mild action: osteopathy, ultra-sonic therapy, infra-red and radiant heat, saunas, steam and sitz baths, various combinations of sweat-inducing bakery: mud, wax, cabinet, peat, blanket baths.

Best of all, massage and manipulation which comes in all possible forms, from pleasurably painful to Wake up, Sir. As I always say, it's nice to be kneaded; but a health farm's asexual: all slap, no tickle.

Looming ominously behind such agreeable time-fillers: enemas and colonic irrigations. Nature cure enthusiasts explain that in decoking the engine, waste poisons must be swept away for a fresh, empty start—and that's the way they gotta go. This may be medically sound but true or false, it's not much fun.

Various spin-off activities, or non-activities, seem more therapeutic: complete rest (or stultifying boredom); non-availability of demoralising distractions, like pleasure; the spiritually uplifting sensation of being above temptation, per force.

I derived additional benefit by giving up smoking 50 a day, on the assumption that if I had to be unhappy anyway, I might as well be utterly miserable. On a fast, mouth coated with dark fur, cigarettes are resistible and the whole system so outraged that one further deprivation goes unnoticed. I commend this ploy to the addicted.

I also—giant stride for one man—cleaned my car. This beneficial, constructive exercise can occupy an afternoon or two. Unfortunately I have had no time for health farms during the past five years, so the car now needs another visit even more than I do.

The Metropole at Brighton recently opened the largest health hydro in Europe. I attended its inaugural week-end; a cheery group drinking mimosas on a private pullman train, inaugural lunch, a week-end of fun and slimming treatment. Without any effort, I put on five pounds.

This hydro may now close, the management realising what anyone as weak-willed as I could have told them before we left Victoria: serious dieting demands monastic seclusion—several thousand acres and long country lanes between you and the nearest steak house. At the Metropole the Other World was down there in the dining-room every night, visibly stuffing, while outside on the promenade, the ice cream bars beckoned . . .

Nature cure is not merely an expensive folly; ignoring its unworldly cancer-cure fringe, the theory seems eminently reasonable: rest, restraint, simple food. The advantage of a farm's outrageous expense is that one may be stunned, upon release into sensible eating. Write off those who triumphantly smuggle scrummy tuck into bedrooms or creep off on afternoon dainty-tea crawls; their weighty problems are here to stay.

The ideal fortnight down on the farm, is ten days' fast (during which you lose a stone) and four days' gentle return, via yoghurt, to salads and plain food; this puts four pounds back into that shrunken stomach. The more flab you take, the more you leave behind; heavy drinkers and the very fat see it drop away, revealing long-lost toes.

Mealtime behaviour after release depends upon your good sense and the impact of the bill. Most edge slowly back to the weight they took with them; sterner souls change their life pattern, better and smaller people for ever.

All right—so I got the car cleaned.

"I'd felt for some time that the cosy old-fashioned type of clinic had had its day."

Songs of Food Production

ABOVE three hundred years ago
  To Britain's shores there came
An immigrant of lineage low—
  Sol Tuberose his name.

He settled down in mean estate,
  Despised on every side,
Until at last he waxed great,
  Grew rich and multiplied.

Now none so popular as he;
  To every house he goes,
At every table he must be—
  The great Sol Tuberose!

In time of war he proves his worth,
  He helps us everywhere;
There's nothing on (or in) this earth
  That can with him compare.

Not the great LLOYD could save the land
  Except for might Sol;
For he is Bread's twin-brother—and
  He gives us Alcohol;

Not such as fills the toper's tum,
  But such as fills the shell—
Such as will be in days to come
  Heat, light, and pow'r as well.

Yes, in the spacious days to come
  We'll bless Sol Tuberose,
When all our motor engines hum
  On what the farmer grows.

Then cultivate him all you can,
  With him and his stand well in;
There's one that is a *Nobleman*,
  There's one *Sir John Llewellyn*.

There's one that is a *British Queen*,
  There's one a dwarf, *Ashleaf*,
There's one that is a plain *Colleen*,
  There's one an *Arran Chief*.

He'll serve us if we do him well
  (Last year he failed our foes).
Oh, who can all the praises tell
  Of good Sol Tuberose!

W.B. 1917

The Health Food Fad
by HEATH

"I don't eat it man—I smoke it."

"Oh him, he's one of my regulars."

"Better make it half a pound—I don't think I could carry a whole pound."

"Ah—the groaning board."

21

ENOUGH IS ENOUGH

CLIVE BARNES,
Drama Critic of the New York Times,
counts the calories

ONE out of every two Americans is overweight. They may not be fat, or that obscene term obese, but they are stocky, pleasantly-rounded, pudgy, well-upholstered, chunky or flabby, according to your way of looking at them. One out of two Americans. No wonder the best-seller lists in America are full of diet books. They are also full of how-to-do-it sex books—so perhaps Americans have other problems too.

In a world of starving, the American nation is buying diet books. At a time of recession Americans are looking at their waistlines. While so many people all over the world are not getting enough to eat, Americans are buying "fake" diet foods where, ideally, all the nutrients have been taken out and all the flavour left in. There is an irony here. In America it is not usually the rich that are fat. It is the rich that are thin. To be rich is to be beautiful, and to be beautiful is to be thin. So just as in Victorian England a healthy paunch to put beneath a gold watch-chain was normally a sign of prosperity, today it is the lean, greyhound look, so skinny that it looks as if a gold watch could even fall off a wrist.

Some people are born fat, some achieve fatness and some have fatness thrust upon them. I happen to belong to all three categories. A childhood tendency to chubbiness was developed with age, and nurtured by profession that has a tendency to be over-social if not over-indulgent. I am one of God's fatties, but, dutifully, every so often, I rebel. I struggle to let the thin man inside me (and I know there is one) get out and I diet. When I diet, my mind is almost obsessed with dieting. I gloat over diet books, I bore family and friends with diet triumphs, failures or even techniques. I also starve, and starve and starve. Even on the diets that claim you can eat as much as you like. Liars.

It was in New York that I went on my first diet. It was 1963, and I was here on a visit. Now at that time I was more cherubic than chubby, but for a 36-year-old I had the air and bearing of a man who could be really fat by the age of 48. New York had just made a magnificent discovery called the drinking man's diet. Everyone was on it—on the Bowery they were knee-deep with its advocates.

I forget the actual details of the diet—in fact I ended up not remembering much of the actual trip. The secret seemed to be that you drank as much as you could and ate very little. The occasional peanut and odd olive I presume—and most olives in New York bars are conveniently odd. This dates the trip because I was drinking what was then known—perhaps just to tourists, but I think not—as

"Vodkatinis". They were simply the same as a Gin Martini made with Vodka, so you finished up seeming stupid rather than smelling drunk. Well, I attacked this diet with vigour. It put weight on me. Better yet, it all but turned me into an alcoholic. I returned to London more cherubic than ever, with my sleech splurred, and very slightly reeling. I think I walked through Heathrow quietly bellowing: "New York, New York is a wonderful town," and not being able to get any further through an inability to remember just what it was that was up and just what it was that was down.

Since then I have tried every diet known to man except bread-and-water in the Tower of London. And diets make me very miserable. Chiefly because after my 1963 experience they involve some degree of water-wagon hopping. If I am none too serious I drink Dry Vermouth on the rocks (which I hate like a roundhead hated Popery) and wine, but if I am really serious I go Cold Turkey—and only wish I could eat the turkey.

Like every badly adjusted fat man in New York, of any intelligence whatsoever, I know more about diet and metabolism than most doctors. The effect of alcohol calories varies enormously from person to person—some lucky people cannot use them, and drinking makes them thin, morose and drunk. Me it makes fat, happy and brilliant. I suppose God meant me to be a Falstaff rather than a Eugene O'Neill. But it is unfortunate. A famous choreographer, a fellow sufferer from "fat-drinks" confided to me the other day: "Man,

"Quite honestly, I don't know why you bother."

23

when I'm dieting, I just have to have one Campari and soda and feel three pounds go on right there."

I have counted calories and I have counted carbohydrates. I have even counted them when, sleepless with hunger and wondering where the next square carrot was coming from, I have been trying to get to sleep. I have eaten protein and nothing but protein and as a supplement drunk eight glasses of water a day. (Eight glasses of water—it reminds one of the famous W. C. Fields roared reply to the tactless hostess who enquired whether he wanted water in his Bourbon: "Water, ma'am, water! Fish fornicate in water!") I once had a diet where I could eat whatever I wanted to eat but had to precede everything with half a grapefruit. It was—if memory serves—called the Grapefruit Diet. I lost a certain faith in it when I noticed that it was sponsored by the Florida Association of Grapefruit Growers—but, of course, for them, it probably worked.

Not all my diets fail. A few memorable years ago, during periods of what we dietitians call the yo-yo effect (with the weight going up and down) I made a desperate effort. I noticed that I weighed 15 stone 10 pounds. No great weight you might say—but not so good if you are only 5' 7" tall. There is certain imbalance there—in fact, you look like one of those Russian Babuska dolls.

Well, I fought the good fight. As I recall it for some time I was taking in nothing but soda water and cottage cheese, reading about the better class restaurants in New York, London and Paris, and thumbing through recipe books to make my mouth water (mind you, by that time it was merely watering soda water) and leafing through the pages of *Punch* and the *New Yorker* gazing reminiscently at all those lovely liquor advertisements in full colour, all featuring happy, thin, laughing people, all clearly on the verge of either seduction at home or promotion at the office. Or, sometimes, both on the beach. And I lost weight. I got down to 10 stones 10 pounds—and felt absolutely marvellous. Happily enough, while returning, in some modified way I suppose, to old habits of ingestion, I more or less held my weight loss for about two years. Then it happened. Quite suddenly, the pounds mounted up like a national debt, and up and up. Three days ago I discovered that I had hit what must be my all time high of 16 stones 6 pounds.

It is a weight at which you feel like a walking advertisement for *Le Guide Michelin*, a weight at which people turn to stare, and a weight at which nervous air-travellers, quite unnecessarily, wonder whether to get off a plane when you get on. It is also, particularly, in New York a weight of shame. A sign of the gourmand rather than the gourmet—even though I had always held that a gourmand was merely a gourmet who had found a good restaurant or delicatessen.

Enough is enough. Three days ago I started to diet once more—if only to be able to cry: "Once more into the breeches, dear friends, once more." Today I lunched at one of New York's best restaurants, sipped Perrier water and ate grilled Dover Sole. Why am I telling you all this? Partly to give myself courage, and partly because, as you must have noticed, all people on a diet are bores, and can talk about nothing else.

"A word of advice—ease up on the health foods."

*"If you're interested in health food,
this is a disposable breakfast cereal.
You simply buy it, take it home and
throw it away."*

Golf Psychiatrist

An American doctor, who claims a high rate of success in lowering golfers' handicaps by psycho-analysis, is opening a clinic in Britain. DAVID LANGDON drives off first.

"I'm at 317 Harley Street—not more than a brassie shot from Baker Street Station."

"Couldn't you tackle it the other way round? Iron out my golf swing and then have a go at my dementia praecox?"

"Could you do us together? She's my partner in the mixed foursomes."

*"Emergency session. He took ten at
the short thirteenth."*

"Try to hold on. There's a psychiatric unit at the 9th."

HOW TO KEEP HEALTHY IN FOG

By a Harley Street Physician

ALL of us at some time or another must have opened our front doors in the morning and found that we were unable to see across the road. Now, when this happens there is no need to panic, or even to seek professional advice. There may be some perfectly simple explanation. We may have mis-set the alarm and got up in the middle of the night. There may be an eclipse. We may have our hat over our eyes. But nevertheless, as any qualified doctor will tell you, it is always wise to think of the possibility of fog.

Patients often ask me: "Doctor, what *is* fog?" Well, the answer is "We don't really know." Like many other physical and mental disorders, we qualified doctors only recognize it by its effects. Doctors are trained to diagnose things like fog from various disconnected signs—fog signals, for instance. Or, if you happen to be near the coast, fog horns. To doctors these signs, particularly if they come together, are almost diagnostic of fog.

The next question is usually a frank one: "What shall I do, doctor, if I begin to suffer from fog myself?" Here we doctors can be a little more definite. If you find yourself in fog the best thing to do is not to breathe at all. Some people, I admit, may find this impracticable. So, if you must breathe, try drawing breaths in places where the fog is less dense. There are plenty of these within reach of everyone. Fog is quite thin in small enclosed spaces like pillar-boxes, for instance. So when you walk down the street draw a deep breath at each pillar-box and hold it to the next one. In areas where pillar-boxes are few and far between, or have been thoughtlessly replaced by wall-type letter slits, try drawing in the breath through the nose—a sharp hissing intake (almost a sniff) is all that is necessary—and expelling it again *immediately* through the mouth. In this way the air, with its dangerous accretions of smoke and tissue-destroying gases, is kept well clear of the lungs. It is only by all of us taking such simple measures as these that the health of our nation can be maintained.

Another thing all of you must be wondering is: "What are you doctors *doing* about fog? Do you think that one day you'll abolish it?"

That's a more difficult one to answer. Doctors have been studying fog now for many years, and we're getting to know a lot about it. We know, for instance, that fog generally slows down the rate of human locomotion. We have noticed that, in fog, people as a whole prefer to spend their time inside their homes rather than out in the street—an interesting piece of sociological research. We also know that fog makes people less able to recognize familiar objects at a distance. From such scattered facts as these we doctors have to piece together the whole picture of fog. This takes time, because we have found that, most unfortunately, fog can be studied only in the winter. But I have one encouraging piece of news: scientists are now evolving a method of creating fog in the summer as well, so that soon we shall be able to study it all the year round.

So next time you think you're suffering from fog, don't worry. And on no account, unless you are a private patient, rush to your doctor at the first slight mist.

"This means a great deal to my wife and I—ecologically speaking that is."

THE NEW HYGIENE

IN view of the paramount importance attached to "fitness" by the best authorities, *Mr. Punch* is happy to announce that he has secured the services of the eminent expert, MR. LEVESON TILES, who will contribute a series of papers of which this is the first instalment.

HOT TO KEEP AWAKE

BY LEVESON TILES, M.A.

The great curse of the age is excess. What excess really is, we do not know, for one man's meat may be another man's poison, and an old proverb—remember that proverbs are the wit of one man but the wisdom of many—lays down the golden rule, "The more the merrier." Still, it may be taken as a postulate of modern life that we sadly ignore the golden mean. We eat too much, drink too much, above all we sleep too much. And as the efficiency of a nation resides in the amount of its output in its waking hours, it stands to reason that the nation which is widest awake must come to the top.

ANTIDOTES TO SOMNOLENCE

First and foremost of the short cuts to wakefulness is the choice of noisy surroundings. Recurrent noises of an identical character are of no use. The men on board a lightship in a fog who are not on duty sleep complacently while the siren hoots every fifteen seconds. Noise to be really stimulating should be irregular and diversified. Thus, if I have an important piece of literary work to finish, I alternate a gramophone with an alarum clock, and by leaving bowls of milk and fragments of fried fish on the leads ensure the attendance of a constant succession of feline serenaders. The Duke of DEVONSHIRE, in his masterly monograph entitled "Wake up, England!" recommends residence in a boiler-maker's yard, or a belfry, but only persons of an iron constitution can stand the strain.

SOME USEFUL RECIPES

Just as the continuous perusal of a serious author is found to promote sleepiness, so the judicious jumping from grave to gay will stave off the insidious overtures of Morpheus. Personally I have derived great benefit from reading a page of HERBERT SPENCER, then a page of *Mrs. Beeton's Cookery Book*, then a page of *Bradshaw*, and so on *da capo*. Alternate sips of barley-water and brandy work marvels with some constitutions, while the excess of blood may be taken from the feet to the brain by filling a hot-water bottle with ice and placing a mustard plaster on the temples. A similar result can also be produced by filling the mouth with capsicums, stinging nettles or red pepper. A jellyfish has in it a certain invigorating quality; so, I believe, has the sea-urchin. Some prefer such things raw; others like them curried. Here is a recipe that might be good for most people, but if anyone feels that it would be improved by the presence of an onion, he can easily add it:—

"Cut off the heads of half a dozen Tandstickor matches, place them in a pan with a solution of oil of nitro-glycerine, stir slowly for half an hour over a slow fire and take what is left to bed."

Another excellent recipe is the patent Kansas folding-up bedstead, which can be set by clockwork to engulf the weary traveller at any specified time. This may be combined with a broken venetian blind with an arc-light outside, and an alarum bell over the bed which signals the arrival of all trains on the Tube and the Inner Circle railway. A hot-water pipe with a hiccough can also be recommended, and by a judicious use of Welsh rarebit, Scotch ale and black coffee, alertness and vivacity may be secured from the most trypanosomatous subject.

PAWLOW recommends early rising. Many people have told me with tears in their eyes that the only effective cure for oversleeping oneself is to get up at 6 A.M. or even sooner. In the words of the great Hibernian philosopher, "the only way to prevent what is past is to put a stop to it before it happens."

THE SELFISHNESS OF SLEEP

But the art of experrection or wakefulness is not solely to be cultivated by attention to physical means. It depends largely on the promotion of an altruistic mentality. Thus one writer, HUDSON JAY, says that the suggestion of vigilance for others, the imagination and realisation of others as alert and wakeful, is the best and sweetest way of securing that condition for yourself.

Sleep, in conclusion, is bound up with selfishness. What you need to do is to turn your attention from the worldly interests of the petty self to the eternal verities of the Kinetic and Cosmic whole. Then, even if wakefulness does not ensue, at any rate the activity of the mind is doing you almost, if not quite, as much good as if you were suffering from chronic insomnia.   1904

"I'm starting hay-fever."

"Thank you Doctor. You do wonders for my fits of depression."

"It's nothing serious, doctor. I'm just feeling superior, that's all."

HOW SICK ARE THE DOCTORS?

RICHARD GORDON Owns Up

MY first experience of enjoying illness "on the house" followed a kick on the head in a football match as a medical student. I woke up in my own hospital to find screens drawn round my bed, from which I concluded I was dead. Then I remembered that, once dead, the nurses stuffed you with cotton-wool at both ends. The only course seemed to feel and find out. I was in a confused state, insisting I suffered not from amnesia but from amenorrhoea, which being the first sign of pregnancy caused a good deal of the hearty jollity bestowed by medical people on their suffering colleagues.

They kept me in for a week's observation, when I fell in love with the night-nurse. Unfortunately, the house-surgeon was in love with her, too, and prescribed me such powerful doses of sedatives I was unconscious almost round the clock. Had the girl not been transferred to another ward, I should undoubtedly have been taken to the theatre to have my skull opened.

Illness to a medical man always brings painful complications spared the layman. "The most tragic thing in the world is a sick doctor," said Shaw—though the most undignified thing would be nearer the mark. This will be readily understandable by people who have been in hospitals themselves, and grasp the essentially military structure of the medical profession.

The doctors are the officers—the specialists of course the generals, who get others to do the dirty work and collect the knighthoods. The nurses are the NCOs, rising from half-scared first-year lance-corporals, still approachable in the right mood, to fire-eating sergeant-majors in blue sisters' dresses. The patients are definitely Other Ranks. And what a pathetic army they are! Rigorously disciplined all their waking and even sleeping hours, confined indefinitely to barracks, never daring to question an order nor make a complaint, deprived of alcohol and sex, hideously uniformed in pyjamas, released only through discharge or death, and as powerless to win promotion as a convict to turn into a warder. For an officer to become a casualty is misfortune enough. To be simultaneously reduced to the ranks is unbearable.

Such crushing humiliation gives doctors the reputation of being bad patients. Admittedly, we become tetchy in a struggle to preserve fragments of self-respect amid bedpans, intramuscular injections, six am washing-bowls, continual television and similar harassments previously imagined as strictly for other people. In fact, we are really subdued and highly co-operative invalids—we don't want to run any risks, having always in mind the fatal possibilities of any disease whatever, not to mention those of most lines of modern treatment.

"That's it then. Swab, suture, overtime claim form."

A consultation between a pair of doctors has the unreal atmosphere of a pair of practised card-sharpers playing a game of poker absolutely straight for fun. Each knows intimately the little tricks and deceptions, even the line of patter, which makes their livelihood possible. Each strives to put them out of mind, and fails as wretchedly as a salesman telling the truth. Doctors are so sensitive about the perfection of their knowledge, the man consulted strains to shake off the mental superiority flowing naturally from his position. The doctor who is the patient tries equally hard to see the other as infallible, which only induces a nauseous feeling of desperation. As both know exactly what the other is thinking, and both distrust each other wildly, they turn the conversation as soon as possible to their families and golf.

Some consultants, like the late Lords Horder and Evans, became so good at this they won the esoteric commendation of being "a doctors' doctor," with huge practices in the profession. Not, of course, that a doctor would ever charge another doctor. If the medical patient recovers, he sends a few bottles of whisky. If he doesn't, it is thought slightly poor form for the consultant to omit sending a wreath.

Sickness being such a social disaster most doctors simply refuse to contemplate it, as the detective never expects to be burgled nor the vicar to go to hell. When it inevitably comes, the illness is taken as an affront, an insult, a stroke of treachery. And death is quite outrageous—a nasty piece of double-dealing by a long-familiar and respected accomplice.

This involved attitude towards disease—of contempt mixed with well-informed fright—leads doctors to see their major complaints as trivial and their minor ones as probably fatal. Thus the most rabid hypochondriacs in the country are all inside the medical profession. I have worried for years over contracting all the more dramatic illnesses in the book, including the psychological ones, until this state of mind is now worrying me deeply. I have, in fact, become quite hypochondriacal about my hypochondria.

If sick doctors get little sympathy from their colleagues they attract even less from their patients. People are delighted to discover their medical advisers to be flesh and blood, with the same unreliability as their own. I don't believe the kindliest of men ever learnt about the death of his doctor without a feeling of smugness. And it is so vexatious for a doctor to be ill when needed by his patients, the public wonder a little resentfully why he can't keep himself healthier than their benighted selves. This would be easier if there were certain laws of health a doctor could follow. Or rather, if they were not constantly changing, like those of modern county cricket.

It is now over twenty years since I gave up cigarettes. I woke one morning with a hangover after a hospital party to find a letter from the Medical Research Council inviting me to send them my smoking habits. They added they would file this away with the utmost care until I dropped dead, when they would put themselves to endless trouble discovering exactly what I had dropped dead of. They have

"Would you mind if I had a second opinion?"

since sent regular little cards asking if the event has yet happened, though whether in hope or encouragement is difficult to tell from the unfailingly cheerful tone of their prose.

I scribbled "No cigarettes" on the letter and sent it back. I turned to cigars, then held by the best statistical opinions as harmless. Unfortunately, this simply meant there weren't enough people in the world who could afford cigars and provide a decent set of figures. By now, the statisticians have collected sufficient cases to prove that cigars are the most lethal smoke of all.

I can't switch to snuff, because they are already rumbling about nasty things happening up the nasal sinuses. I should like to give up smoking altogether and eat bars of chocolate, but everyone knows that fat people perish with alarming ease. Or rather, everyone knows it in the present state of medical knowledge. I should not be surprised if in a few years the statisticians discover that only overweight cigarette chain-smokers have the secret of longevity.

As one must start somewhere, I have drawn up four rules of health, which I would press on the public:

1. Don't smoke cigarettes.
2. Keep your weight down.
3. Take regular exercise.
4. Look both ways before stepping off the pavement.

The last will probably be the most enduring. Doctors may differ, but drivers can be relied on to stay the same.

*"What we both need is a
forty-hour week."*

UNGENERAL PRACTICES

WILLIAM HEWISON applies his rubber hammer to a rare group of knees

This young GP is always the same—cheerful, breezy, bouncy. Go to his morning surgery and when you get in to see him he'll chat away to you about anything and everything—floating off into conversational by-ways whenever you want to tell him why you are there. Eventually you do get the salient facts through to him; in return you receive a prescription and a tremendous dose of reassurance. As you go out through the door you leave all your anxieties behind.

His first week with the Practice and here he is on the morning round—his acres of ignorance staring him in the face. For the moment he is having to hide behind the "I'm-afraid-I've-left-my-prescription-pad-at-the-surgery" ploy. Gives him a little time to consult his books and/or his senior partner.

"No, I was never struck off—that was a malicious rumour and I am fully aware who started it. Her and her Temperance League! It's untrue, also, that I have not kept up with developments—don't I get a hundredweight of pharmaceutical samples each week and don't I try them out on my patients? Those who haven't deserted me for that young whippersnapper at the top of the village, that is. Antibiotics? I'd put my money on a decent glass of old port any time."

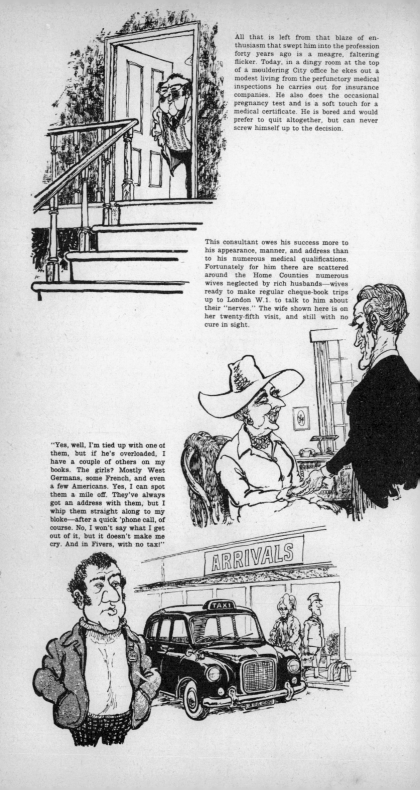

All that is left from that blaze of enthusiasm that swept him into the profession forty years ago is a meagre, faltering flicker. Today, in a dingy room at the top of a mouldering City office he ekes out a modest living from the perfunctory medical inspections he carries out for insurance companies. He also does the occasional pregnancy test and is a soft touch for a medical certificate. He is bored and would prefer to quit altogether, but can never screw himself up to the decision.

This consultant owes his success more to his appearance, manner, and address than to his numerous medical qualifications. Fortunately for him there are scattered around the Home Counties numerous wives neglected by rich husbands—wives ready to make regular cheque-book trips up to London W.1. to talk to him about their "nerves." The wife shown here is on her twenty-fifth visit, and still with no cure in sight.

"Yes, well, I'm tied up with one of them, but if he's overloaded, I have a couple of others on my books. The girls? Mostly West Germans, some French, and even a few Americans. Yes, I can spot them a mile off. They've always got an address with them, but I whip them straight along to my bloke—after a quick 'phone call, of course. No, I won't say what I get out of it, but it doesn't make me cry. And in Fivers, with no tax!"

ARRIVALS

TAXI

ON A CLEAR DAY YOU CAN SAW FOR EVER

The Christian Barnard Story

starring

Christian Barnard as fun-loving playboy
Christian Barnard

and as world-famed surgeon Dr. Barnard featuring 16 new smash-hit operations (soon available from your local hospital) in glorious South Africa colour, so to speak.

(*A medical laboratory somewhere in South Africa, land of opportunity and sunshine. Two young doctors, Barnard and Kloofstein, are sitting at their benches while the lab assistants move round them with all the grace of dancers dressed temporarily in white coats. Barnard sighs and looks up from his rat.*)

Barnard: You know something, Kloofstein?

Kloofstein: I wouldn't say that exactly. Still, I did pass my South African medical exam and that must prove something.

Barnard: You mean, it proves you're a white man?

Kloofstein: Sure, and didn't I know that already? But I had the divil of a job explaining away me suntanned Irish grandmother.

Barnard: Oh, really?

Kloofstein: No, O'Reilly. She came here in 1922 because she didn't like the sound of the Black and Tans. Tans she could take at a pinch, but . . .

(*The laboratory assistants break into a frenzied dance in honour of South Africa's booming industry and standard of living, details on request from your nearest South Africa house.*)

Barnard: You know something, Kloofstein?

Kloofstein: Well, yes, but promise not to tell the police?

Barnard: When I became a surgeon, I never thought it would lead to this life of drudgery. Here I am, already twenty-two years old with a wife and grown-up daughter, and condemned to a routine existence in the operating theatre. (*sings*)

> I've excavated stomachs
> And tried lobotomy,
> I've mastered all the old tricks
> (But see Appendix B).
>
> I'm tired of digging gallstones
> As big as diamonds,
> I'm even tired of probing
> The guts of gorgeous blondes.
>
> Now what I need is a new operation,
> Something involving false kneecaps, maybe,
> Or ivory funny bones—anything, anything,
> Provided it throws all the limelight on me,

41

On me and South Africa, land of equality,
Despite what they say in the overseas press
(So just send a postcard for colourful details
Stating your biases, name and address).

You see, Kloofstein, I've just got to *do* something. It's no good sitting in a small South African hospital being drooled over by student nurses. I want to be drooled over by girls everywhere!

Kloofstein (*suddenly excited*): Hey, look at this, Christian! You know those two mice we experimented with in the tea-break—just swapped their stomachs over to see what would happen?

Barnard: Yes? What did happen?

Kloofstein: They're dead.

Barnard: Of course they are. It was all right as operations go but it failed because it didn't have any publicity. *That's* what we need. The difference between two dead mice and a surgical breakthrough is a press conference. (*The corps de ballet take out pads and pencils and strike an attentive pose.*) Gentlemen, we have made medical history in this morning's tea-break. We have transplanted a wart from one mouse to another. This also means of course that we have transplanted an entire mouse from one wart to another. Are there any questions?

Leading dancer: How soon do you think it will be before you can graft a mouse-wart on to man?

Barnard: Well, I shall be working through my lunch-break.

Kloofstein: Wake up, Christian—you're dreaming. Those two mice are dead and no amount of publicity can bring them back now. Face the facts of life, man.

Barnard: I don't know, though. That stomach graft has given me an idea. I wonder . . .

"*Don't worry, Sister! He can't get far without a heart!*"

(*And so for the next few years Dr. Barnard grafts away in his laboratory, moving organs from one small mammal after another and into the most exciting places. There are setbacks; when a dog escapes from the lab and runs miaowing through the neighbourhood, a surly mob of peasants armed with pitchforks march on his quarters and are only pacified by his spectacular rendition of "Old Man Liver". But at last his work is complete and he presents himself to the South African Health Dept.*)

Dr. Van der Graaft: Gentlemen, may I introduce Dr. Barnard to you? (*A quick vote is taken, the result being fifteen in favour and one against. The dissenter is quickly arrested under the Ninety Day regulations and never seen again.*) Gut. I mean, good. Now, Dr. Barnard, will you briefly explain this revolutionary new operation you have been rehearsing?

Barnard: Of course. As you all know, foreign surgeons have learnt to replace almost every part of the human body with new substitutes. However, there is one organ that has never, in the whole history of surgery, been replaced. When the heart dies, its owner dies with it. (*Growing more and more animated.*) All I need is faith and money, and if you grant me your faith and your money I maintain that I can prove—yes, *prove*—that somewhere beyond the Atlantic Ocean lies the fabled land of Cathay, where untold wealth and treasure . . .

Van der Graaft: I don't quite follow . . .

Barnard: That is to say, I can now *transplant a heart from one man to another*. (*There is a long silence.*)

Surgeon: Is that *all*?

2nd Surgeon: It doesn't seem enough for a whole act, does it?

3rd Surgeon: I remember old Dr. Blitzfontein doing something very like that at our student socials.

4th Surgeon: But he could do the Charleston at the same time.

5th Surgeon: *And* balance a gallstone on his nose.   ..

Van der Graaft: Thank you for coming along, Dr. Barnard—we'll let you know.

Barnard: But don't you realise? What I propose is an operation that could put South Africa at the top again! It would mean fame, acceptance, international respect, even a new heart for somebody! (*The surgeons confer briefly.*)

Van der Graaft: All right, Barnard, we'll give you your chance. We're putting you on for a four-week run at the old Groote Schur theatre. If your idea turns out to be a solid, respectable, long-term piece of medical research, you're fired—if the crowds love it, you're in.

(*Four weeks later. Dr. Barnard sits in his office at Groote Schur, putting fan letters in the waste paper basket. Some of them he sniffs at and places aside. Van der Graaft enters.*)

Van der Graaft: My dear fellow! You did it! You are famous!

Barnard: Oh, it was nothing really.

Van der Graaft: Of course, but we must let nobody know that. Mind if I sit down? All those stairs, you know.

Barnard: You feeling all right? Heart not playing you up?

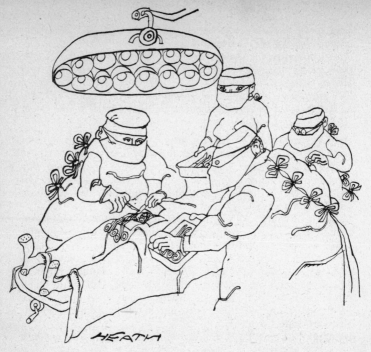

"He contains artificial flavouring, vegetable colouring, albumen, plus additives . . . "

Van der Graaft: Don't touch me, you fiend! Take your vampire hands off me or I'll have you arrested for your devilish practices!

Barnard: No offence, I'm sure!

Van der Graaft: Well, one taken then. Now, as you know, we always like to have a South African celebrity touring the world to prove that our political system is the best possible or, at the very least, that we do grant passports to one or two people. For various reasons the Springbok rugby team is not quite the symbol it used to be so we thought you might like to take the job on instead and that's an order.

Barnard: You want *me* to play against New Zealand?

Van der Graaft: No, I want you to step from obscurity to stardom overnight, Christian. It'll mean leaving your life's work behind—no more propping patients up at press conferences, no more scanning the latest road accident news, no more "Dr. Barnard's Homes—No Donor Ever Turned Away" . . .

Barnard: I'll pack my sunglasses and pyjama tops right away.

Van der Graaft: Good. You leave tonight for a photo-call with Gina Lollobrigida or the Pope. I expect you'd prefer Gina?

Barnard: Certainly. I'd hate to meet someone else who claimed to be top Christian. (*Van der Graaft claps him on the shoulders and leaves.*) Well! If only old Kloofstein could see me now! (*Dr. Kloofstein passes the window and glances in without much interest.*) Not that I won't be sorry to leave the place. (*Sings*)

I left my heart in Groote Schur,
Just lying on the desk—
When I got back, they'd put the thing
In someone else's chest.

Ich hab mein Herz in Groote Schur verloren,
Through lending it to Dr. You-know-who.
He said they wouldn't want it for much longer,
But till then they'd need my lungs and kidneys too.

Groote Schur, Groote Schur, Groote Schur
Is the Afrikaans for "Take off your shirt,
You're about to become world-famous.
If you do what you're told, it won't hurt."

(*Several years have passed. Dr. Barnard has become more famous, richer, younger, more handsome, even if his patients have not. Shortly after the last transplant subject has died, he is sitting in an outlying district of his sitting-room. Dr. Kloofstein comes in.*)

Kloofstein: Dr. Barnard?
Barnard (*not looking up*)**:** Just leave your heart on the table, will you?
Kloofstein: It's me, Christian—Dr. Kloofstein.
Barnard: Jan! How are you? After all these years! Just leave your heart on the table, will you?
Kloofstein: I'm glad you remember the time we spent together cutting up mice. And now you're world-famous, while I . . .
Barnard: Yes?
Kloofstein: Oh, I'm sole concessionaire of rats and mice for South African laboratories—it's not much of a life, but it's left me a millionaire.
Barnard: That's marvellous! Now, what can I do for you?
Kloofstein: I want you to do an operation. It's my first cousin once removed on my Irish side, Martha. She could be a great singer, Christian, one of the greatest, but she has this very weak heart and the doctors only give her a year.
Barnard: Jan, there's no one I'd rather swap hearts for, but it's not that simple. You see, I haven't actually done an operation for years and I've started wondering if I'm the surgeon I used to be. (*He stares down at his fingers; his fingers stare back at him.*) I'd never forgive myself if anything . . .
Kloofstein: It's her only chance . . .
Barnard: It's a big thing to ask . . .
Kloofstein: You're the only person I can turn to . . .

(*The same a month later.*)

Kloofstein: Well, Christian, your name is on every front page!
Barnard: It's good to feel that I'm a surgeon again at last.
Kloofstein: Surgeon? You're the greatest in the world!
Barnard: It's nice of you to say so, Jan. There's only one thing I'm sorry about—I wish your cousin could be here with us.

Kloofstein: Please don't worry about that, Christian. Even the greatest operations can be complete failures.

Barnard: I suppose you're right. Anyway, she can live to sing again in the film.

Kloofstein: Film?

Barnard: Haven't you heard? I'm starring in my own life.

Kloofstein: That's wonderful! And you'll be needing lots of rats and mice for it, I imagine.

Barnard: Lots of girls . . .

Kloofstein: Lots of money . . .

Together: All you really need is hearts,
Rats and girls and loot and hearts . . .

(*In unison they tap-dance their way out of the film and into our hearts.* Blood by Heinz, script research by **MILES KINGTON**.)

"*As one specialist to another, Horringer, how do you cope with the problem of monotony?*"

...MEANWHILE, BACK AT THE RANCH-STYLE SPLIT-LEVEL SURGERY...

ARNOLD ROTH ups stethoscope and draws his bead on a few Stateside MDs

The "referral" routine is common medical procedure. This man has come to a General Practitioner . . .

. . . because of his post-nasal drip. The doctor refers him to an old school friend specialist . . .

. . . whose speciality is gall bladders and who refers the man . . .

. . . to a special specialist partner whose job is to refer him on to . . .

. . . a neuro-surgeon cousin who removes the man's left leg then . . .

. . . refers him to a burial-plot-salesman-nephew . . . (just in case) . . . who refers him . . .

. . . to a brother-in-law who sells shoes in singles and . . .

. . . notices the man's post-nasal trouble and refers him to his wife's uncle . . .

. . . who is a very sincere physician who refers . . .

Blood Money

A day in the life of Dr. KEITH WATERHOUSE

"The Government should order doctors to stop over-prescribing if it wants to cut the cost of medicines, leading chemists said yesterday."—*Daily Telegraph*

YOUNG Shirley Neverwell was worried about her complexion, as well she might have been. She was a deep yellow in hue, which was leading her workmates to call her Buttercup.

"Still at the match factory? I asked. "I thought so. You've got phossy jaw."

"That's what old Dr. Goodenough used to tell me," volunteered Shirley. "He always used to prescribe copper sulphate ($1\frac{1}{2}$-3 grains) as an emetic."

"Yes, well I'm afraid those days are over, Shirley," I said. "Do you know how much copper sulphate is fetching per ton on the open market? Stick your finger down your throat, there's a good girl. And for God's sake go and get a job in Woolworth's."

Neville Heath Neverwell is one of my regulars. Hardly an evening surgery goes by without he doesn't pop in complaining of some little ache and pain or other. This time it was haemoglobinuria, jaundice, fever, vomiting, and severe haemolysis.

"Spleen and liver enlarged, are they?" I asked. "Epigastric discomfort? Passing port-wine-coloured urine?"

Neville nodded.

"I thought as much," I said. "Black-water fever."

The old-fashioned treatment for Neville's trouble is absolute rest, plenty of alkaline fluids, blood transfusion, and glucose given intravenously. But I thought I'd try a little experiment.

"Here's a prescription for a bottle of Lucofizz on sale or return," I said. "Take three tablespoons a day and try to keep out of draughts, Central Africa, India and the Far East."

That was four weeks ago and Neville hasn't been back since. Either black-water fever has taken its toll or he's pocketed the threepence back on the Lucofizz bottle, which of course by rights belongs to the National Health.

Lady Eleanour de Gray Beaufort Neverwell wasn't too put out when her youngest, the Hon. Cedric, swallowed a new penny. He's a rare one for sucking coins of the realm, and over the years he has acquired something of a local reputation as a walking piggy-bank.

"Old Dr. Goodenough believed in nature taking its course," confided Lady E. "As a general rule he would recommend a little syrup of figs to help things along."

"Figs," I had to tell her, "do not grow on trees. I shall have to operate. How much currency is within the little shaver as of even date?"

"I wish you'd called me sooner, Mrs. Moodie."

"About 25p, some of it in old money," she reported.
"Finders keepers," I said.

For as long as I've been in practice Francisco de Isturiz Neverwell, SJ, has been asking for what we in the medical profession call a bunch of fives.

He suffers, you see, from digital poisoning, which is brought on by taking medicine in excessive doses. Francisco's heartbeat was slow and irregular, he had been having convulsions, and he was, at the time he was wheeled into my surgery on a handcart, unconscious.

All this was brought on by swigging, in vast quantities, weak potassium permanganate solution which is supposed to be the remedy for the very complaint I have just described.

"You're in a vicious circle, Francisco, lad," I advised him, burning a few feathers under his nose. "You do realise, I hope, that the leading chemists have got up a petition against you and your extravagant ways?"

"Old Dr. Goodenough," he gasped, "used to give me blank prescription forms and leave me to fill them in myself."

"You know perfectly well," I replied, "that old Dr. Goodenough has just been struck off for over-prescribing liniment of camphor to immigrants who use it as a basis for a very dry cocktail. I'm giving you two asprins and I want you to suck them, not crunch them."

I had to climb on my high horse when Queen Juliana Neverwell, who suffers from hereditary microcytic hypochromic anaemia, dropped into the surgery.

"Brittle nails you may have as a result of your condition," I exploded. "But if you think you are getting Revlon Crystalline Spunsugar Pink nail varnish on prescription, thus placing leading chemists in the embarrassing position of having to rat on their superior colleagues, you have got to be out of your skull. And furthermore," I went on, "there is enough preparation of ferrous sulphate left in this bottle to keep a family of five on 200 to 400 mg thrice daily for the rest of their lives. Kindly get out of my sight."

Glubb Pasha Neverwell of that Ilk is a martyr to nervous diseases. Since my Black's Medical Dictionary was due back at the public library shortly before he dropped in to see me, I was unable to pinpoint his symptoms more closely than that.

I do know, however, that old Dr. Goodenough was a fool to himself in prescribing phenobarbitone sodium, allobarbitone, butobarbitone, amylobarbitone, pentobarbitone, cyclobarbitone, hexobarbitone, quinalbarbitone and headache powders in quantities sufficient to make it worth young Neverwell's while to have them carted away in a lorry.

"I'm putting you on Pontefract Castle Toffee Assortment, Glubb," I explained. I didn't bother to tell him that these are what we medicoes call a placebo; they're available from all reputable confectioners at 10p a quarter, and if they don't keep you out of the dentist's at least they keep you out of the leading chemists, except for an emergency issue of cotton-wool soaked in a mixture of chloral and menthol, which is nothing whatever to do with me.

The Rt. Hon. Plantagenet Berkeley Arbuthnot Neverwell, Pretender to the Ancient Throne of Wessex, is a bit of a malingerer between you and me. He does in fact have a touch of coal miner's lung, Kümmell's Disease, gout, fatty degeneration of the heart, paralysis of the abducent nerve, hernia, misplaced sternum, St. Anthony's Fire, neurasthenia, Mediterranean fever, gall-stones, dyspepsia, ringworm of the beard, mushroom poisoning, simple enlargement of the thyroid gland, lead colic, bromidrosis, impetigo, botulism and chapped hands, but as I keep telling him, so who's perfect?

"You're a good customer, Plantagenet," I said, "and I'm offering you first lick of the spoon that old Mrs. Wilkinson, God rest her soul, has been using for her liver extract."

"No deal," he replied, all hoity-toity. "When old Dr. Goodenough was here it was out with the trade samples from ICI, Boots, all the big names—one month's prescription on approval, perm any five from six."

"We live in changing times," I told him. "Let's save the taxpayer a few bob and put you on Frenkel's Exercises, to be performed by patients having difficulty in controlling their muscles."

"But I need medicine, doctor! There's nothing wrong with my muscles."

"There will be," I said, "if you don't get out of here and stop wasting public money."

"Relax! Mr. Yamahaka, relax."

BUPAMAN

GRAHAM is admitted to the private wing

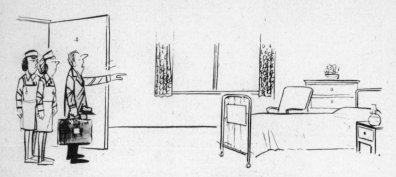

"*Right! We'll have the bed nearer the window for a start.*"

"*I'm sandwiched between a Greek
ship-owner with gallstones and a sheikh
who fell off his horse.*"

"*At two hundred and forty quid a week
I was expecting something prettier.*"

"*Now look, Sir Thomas, or whatever your name is . . .*"

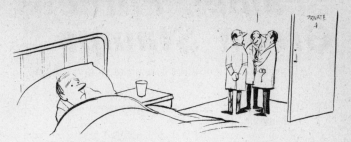

"*No doubt about it—a severe attack of loneliness.*"

"*Should I tip the surgeon,
d'you think?*"

"*Have you noticed how their temperatures
vary with the Financial Times Index?*"

"*But I don't want to go home! I like it here!*"

Scalpel, Forceps, Green Stamps...

ALEN COREN samples free enterprise medicine

"THE doctor will see you now," said the receptionist.

"Thank you," I said.

"That'll be a pound," she said, as I hobbled beside her from the waiting-room to the surgery.

"What?"

"You should've been after Mrs. Foskett," she said, "really. The stingy mare."

I passed the note across. She ogled, and poked an armoured breast against my upper arm.

"Do you a nice colonic," she murmured. "Any Sunday. Only a fiver, including music."

"I've come about the sprain," I said.

"*Stereo* music. There's not every SRN got a Bang and Olufsen. I'm not just a big bust, you know."

"I think my colon's all right," I said.

She tossed her ginger ringlets.

"One of those, are you?" she said. She rapped on the glass door. "Come in!"

The doctor was standing by the window, staring out.

"Look at that!" he muttered, not turning. I limped across, and he pulled the curtain aside. Opposite, above a plate-glass window full of plump little corpses, a signwriter was just finishing off: JAS. BENBOW & SONS, HIGH CLASS POULTERERS & SURGEONS. LET US QUOTE YOU.

"What a diabolical liberty!" cried the doctor. "Opening up opposite!"

"Is he qualified?" I asked.

"If you want your neck wrung," said the doctor, "you couldn't go to a better bloke. I don't know what it's coming to! Do you know how long it took me to train?"

I shook my head.

"Eight months!" he cried. "Eight months of study, no pay, up all night with the skeleton, nice little tobacconist's going to pot downstairs, you can't expect a woman to recommend pipes, can you? I took medicine seriously, that's the way I am; quick, what am I holding up?"

"A finger?"

"I thought you'd say that, yes, it may be a finger to the layman, but it's a digit to me, that's the trade name and there's a lot more like that, I had nearly fifty pages to read up, what's the function of the pancreas?"

"I don't know," I said, "About my sprain—."

"I don't know either," said the doctor; he turned again, and threw open the window. "BUT AT LEAST I DON'T CALL IT BLOODY SWEETBREADS!" he screamed. He hurled the window down once more.

"Well, then?" he said.

"I think I've sprained my ankle."

"Got a Special on boils this week," said the doctor. "I lance two for a tenner, you get the third one free."

"I don't think I have any boils."

"I'd have a good look if I were you, squire. It's an unrivalled opportunity. Normally a fiver apiece." He snapped open his bag and withdrew an abacus. "Take your clothes off."

"Do I have to?"

He shrugged.

"Might as well, it's included. Get a bit of fresh air on your body, if nothing else." He passed me a heavily stained tryptich, and flipped it open. "Now, if I may make a suggestion, squire, why don't you start with a small ear examination, that's always very popular—syringing is extra, of course—then go on to a nice bit of stethoscoping with a little gland-feel on the side, follow that with our Business-man's Throat Bargain, which is two Aaahs, five seconds flashlight, spatula and spit, and finish up with a quick prostate probe and cough. Can't go wrong for £6.50, plus VAT, cost you a pony down the Middlesex and they won't even warm their fingers first."

"Forgive me, but how will that help my sprain?"

"Sprain, sprain, why do I get all the bloody hypochondriacs? Look, son, I don't do à la carte stuff, not worth it, see what I mean,

"One of his bloody private patients I suppose."

55

"It's my first epidemic."

I'd have to read up God knows what, start laying out money on all kinds of gear, ophthalmoscopes, litmus paper, bunsen burners, one of them little rubber hammers, I'm not made of money, am I, I do two menus, the 6.50 plus and the 8.50 plus—that's where you also get to pee in the jam jar and read the wall-card—and that's it. I find it covers ninety per cent of cases, take the brown medicine after every meal, go to bed, if it's not better by morning, try the bloke next door, he does acupuncture, splints, VD and blackheads. Or there's Jas. Bleeding Benbow across the road, he'll turn you into ten chump chops for a fiver and throw in a stuffed shoulder as well. I mean, streamlining, that's the secret of the small business, right, process-rationalisation, the bulk of my patients are quite happy to drop in, have a wee-wee in the receptacle provided, enquire about my unbeatable Haemorrhoid Insurance Scheme, go 'Ninety-nine', and take away a bottle of the cherry-flavoured brown."

I reached for my underpants.

"I think I'd like a second opinion," I said, "thanks very much."

A door opened behind him.

"Pregnant," said a small dark man in a bloodstained boiler suit. "Congratulations."

"What?" I said.

"You wanted a second opinion," said the doctor. "You got a second opinion. He's my partner."

"Also windows cleaned," said the small dark man. "Yes, you're about five months gone, I'd say. We can fix it though. Who's the father?"

"I'm a man," I said.

"All right, then, who's the mother?"

"You don't seem to understand," I said, "I have sprained my ankle."

"I see," said the small dark man. "This could be serious. You could lose the baby."

"Nine pounds fifty," said the first doctor. "Used notes, if it's all the same."

"What for?" I cried.

"What for? *What for?* All those bloody consultations, that's what for! Right, Dennis?"

"Right! I'll sprain your other bloody leg, mate! *And* so's no-one'd notice. I know the human body like the back of my wossname."

"He used to be with St. John's Ambulance," said the first doctor. "He's seen more village fêtes than you've had hot dinners."

I passed the money across. They fought over it for a while, then pocketed the remains.

"Okay," said the small dark man, "here's what you do. Drink a bottle of gin and get in a hot bath. You've been a silly girl."

"Or go for a long ride on a horse," said his partner.

I limped out again.

"You've got a lovely body," said the receptionist. "What about a little assisted osteopathy?"

"No, thank you," I said.

"You wouldn't lose work-time. I practise in a Volkswagen. You wouldn't even have to take your hat off. I plug my vibro into the roof-light."

"Goodbye," I said.

"There's a radio," she called after me.

I slammed the door and crossed the street. Jas. Benbow was standing outside his shop, a stethoscope over his blue-and-white striped apron. He took his straw boater off as I passed, and narrowed an eye expertly.

"I'd have that sprain off if I was you," he said.

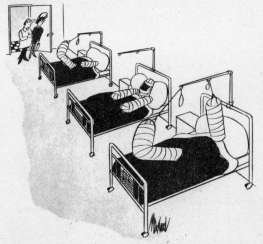

"We are waiting for the return of our private patients."

What Price the Hippocratic Oath?

CHRISTINE PICKARD

I USED to wonder why I was never taken very seriously in my role as a doctor (by those who didn't know me, I hasten to add). There was no question of judging by results: my patients were in the habit of summing me up—the stranger in their midst—within the first half-hour. There was a puzzled look in their eyes, an almost visible shaking of heads. True I didn't really look the part. I was too young and "with-it" for that.

Invariably I retaliated by parading my regalia: stethoscope, sphygmomanometer, came out with a flourish. Finally, I countered with my prescription pad; at this point the fencing usually stopped—one more duel to my credit.

I left each house enveloped in a sad bewilderment. What could I do? I had always been a fanatic for communication, made a point of telling patients exactly how and what was wrong. Always done gently of course, careful not to deal any unnecessary blows. It became a fine art: no long words, absolutely no mystique. I always talked as if I were a next door neighbour. Now my blunder is all too clear. People need the mystique. Even I, who ought to know better, like to put blind faith in the superior knowledge of my medical attendant when I am ill. I hereby apologise to my erstwhile patients for not playing the game; how I must have deprived you. A few long words, muttering the word Hippocrates under my breath and all could have been well.

MADAME MYSTIQUE

Ah, but there's the rub. Hippocrates isn't quite one of my pet hates, but at the mention of his oath, adverse reaction certainly sets in.

To me it smacks of nothing more than a big confidence trick. However, I do realise that it helps patients to believe in doctors: and this, as I have just explained, is paramount. By the same token, it eases the physician's task.

So, if you are about to be ill, please stop reading or dire consequences might result. I certainly won't answer for any damage to your doctor-patient relationship. On the other hand, if you are pretty hale and hearty there is a good chance you'll be able to forget the following paragraphs by the time you fall sick as, indeed, I can myself when the pressure is on.

First of all then, doctors do not swear the Hippocratic oath, nor anything remotely resembling it. At no stage of the medical course was there so much as a bleep about ethics, not even a passing reference to the honour attached to our calling and medicine's supposed status as a vocation patently ignored. We absorbed the facts, passed our exams and were duly "let loose on the public".

I must admit I half expected some cryptic notice to appear, warning us of the responsibilities ahead as the degree day ceremony approached; perhaps some learned gent would spring a list of responses upon us that we would be forced to utter at the final hour.

Or is some Latin sentence (actually it might have been in Greek) supposed to endow the newly graduated doctor with a special moral sense?

Ever since I qualified I have been regaled with comments such as "Ah! But you swore the Hippocratic oath," as if that completely changed everything. This sort of remark is supposed to represent the last word on the subject: the speaker will brook no disagreement at that point. With good grace I try to tolerate the somewhat larger than life aura with which I am endowed. I am raised above mere mortals, automatically incapable of doing any mean, dishonest or truly selfish act. What rot! Yet even scientists and, I am ashamed to say, a few doctors as well, fall into the trap. At the recent inaugural meeting of the British Society for Social Responsibility in Science, it was widely felt that if only scientists had their very own Hippocratic oath chaining them to the straight and narrow, all would be well and all abuse of scientific discoveries would practically cease.

Besides, Hippocrates himself did not write the oath. He believed, as far as we know, in infanticide, euthanasia and in providing the means for suicide for the incurably ill. This is in direct contrast to the tone of the oath which emphasises the preservation of life at all times. There is also no doubt that this supposed paragon of all medical virtues was highly conscious of the profit motive in his dealings with the sick.

It was actually the followers of Pythagoras, the famous mathematician, who formed a break-away philosophical group who devised the oath, probably as a symbol of group unity. It resembles a club manifesto, and the overwhelming impression gained from reading it is the importance of loyalty towards one's fellow physicians. Therefore, in writing at all, I am breaking its cardinal rule.

What is more, Hippocrates, who is so admired as the father of medicine, most likely only wrote four of the seventy books on medical matters traditionally attributed to him. Or, he might have written none at all. What is more, he was first and foremost a bonesetter—an osteopath. Yet, the profession itself still persists in cold shouldering osteopathy, despite its long traditions and connections with the "master".

Last, but not least, the oath is surely incompatible with any form of Christian society. It starts off: "I swear by Apollo Physician and Asclepius and Hygieia and Panacea and all the gods and goddesses . . ." How the oath ever gained its present status defeats me. Perhaps because it fosters the image of the doctor as a "high priest" able to dispense the "sacraments" of health. However, if it ever fell from favour, could we possibly fill the gap?

"He says he wants his teeth fixed on the National Health."

THE
IATROGENIC DISEASE

Olga Franklin

I WENT to my doctor with an ear-ache but he said it was my teeth. The dentist said it wasn't my teeth but it could be my imagination.

In the end I found out what was wrong from a newspaper article. It said that a certain Dr Gibson got up at a British Medical Association conference recently and said that people were getting to be more diseased than ever before. He said hardly anyone was free of something he called "the iatrogenic disease".

At first I didn't know he was referring to me and my ear-ache. But I'm always very interested in illnesses and things like that. I hadn't got the ear-ache any more, but it could well be that I had this "iatrogenic" thing (did it hit the liver or the stomach?) so I was going through *Black's* and three other medical dictionaries, as well as some old copies of the *Lancet* we've got in our library. Sometimes you get the most interesting letters written to the *Lancet*, especially from doctors with patients with mystery diseases. You can pick up the most strange information.

But I couldn't find the iatrogenic disease in *Black's* or anywhere. Which was worrying. Because, how do you know you haven't got it, if you don't know what the symptoms are?

So in the end I had to go to the doctor with it, and he said I'd got it from *him*. He took me to the door of his surgery and opened it a crack. There were about eighteen people sitting there, looking rather well I thought. "They've all got it," said the doctor in a somewhat nasty whisper. He said people got it from going to the doctor too often and from swallowing too many tablets and tranquillisers and pills and things. He said Iatros was a Greek word meaning Doctor and that's why this disease was described at the British Medical Association Conference as being a doctor-induced illness.

Was there a cure then? "Ah," said the doctor, "you're not catching me with that one!" He said I should go home and look in my medicine cabinet and work out the cure for myself.

I'm one of those people who always do what the doctor orders. So I went home and unloaded the medicine phials and bottles to see what would happen.

That was, I think, when my cure started. There was a quantity of stuff for mosquito bites. I'd got a selection of five different coloured stuff, liquid, spray-on and just plain anti-bite creams. I remember the doctor had made the most intensive series of tests for my various

allergies. Then there were my anti-sneeze pills, headache stuff, asthma pills and so on and so on.

I think it was the sight of those almost-forgotten unused asthma pills that started my cure. However did I come to get asthma? Was I cured or had I still got it? One day the doctor said, in a tired sort of way, that if the pills didn't cure me, it could be I had some obscure nervous asthmatic condition. That must have been the day I caught asthma, "iatrogenically" speaking.

I counted all the little bottles, mostly more than half or three-quarters full. There was no clue what they were intended to cure or to sedate or to tranquillise. It was clear, however, that I must be pretty far gone, with this lot. Could I be saved, or was it already too late for that?

The funny thing was that I suppose all the ailments must have got better of their own accord. Because it didn't look as though I'd taken much of a swig at the medicine bottles. Here and there, a few tablets were missing from a box or phial. And some of the bottles of stuff had shrunk a bit, or anyway sort of evaporated. I always did try to swallow one or two of the pills, just to show willing. It's not fair to the doctor otherwise. But I confess I found some pills made me a bit sleepy or a bit "high"; some really didn't taste very nice; some were too big to swallow and I had to spit them out.

I hope I'm not a hypochondriac or anything like that. Surely not? Why, there was one time I'd gone a whole two months without going to see the doctor. Besides everybody knew that it was these regular check-ups that kept you fit! I remember way back, about 1947, I'd heard someone say the very same thing—right in the Ministry of Health itself. It was during a press conference and the Minister spoke.

Some reporter got up and asked him: "Please Minister, what is your answer to the suggestion made that a National Health Service with free treatment by doctors and free medicine, could turn us all into a nation of hypochondriacs?"

Mr Aneurin Bevan, I recall, was a bit sharp in reply. I remember him saying that if the reporter had ever worked in a mine in South Wales and coughed his lungs out afterwards, he wouldn't ask such damn silly questions. In future, the Minister said, people wouldn't die of coughs and things like that because you could go to your free doctor and get it stopped before it got that bad.

At the time I thought Nye was so right. But now I'm not so sure. Look at my own beastly cough, for example, and this mysterious ear-ache thing. I've never been near a coalmine either. I've only been near my nice, kind attractive doctor . . . perhaps a bit too often. How was I to know that's where I'd pick up the infection? No one ever told me, before this Dr Gibson mentioned it, that you could get an ear-ache from going to the doctor.

A LITTLE OF WHAT YOU FANCY

How far does medicine help those who help themselves ?

BRIAN INGLIS examines the placebo-effect

TOWARDS the end of the last century—the story runs—Emile Coué, then a chemist's apprentice, observed that a medicine his employer prescribed for a patient had highly beneficial results. Intrigued, he analysed it, and found it to be coloured water. From this, Coué evolved his theory of auto-suggestion; and eventually, all over the world, people began muttering his incantation "every day, in every way, I get better and better." The medical profession, however, was not impressed; and gradually Couéism sank into oblivion.

Then, in the early 1930s, Evans and Hoyle produced a paper for which posterity will award them—and Coué—a belated accolade. In it, they described how they had discovered that treatment with a dummy pill had satisfactorily relieved the symptoms of over a third of a group of patients suffering from angina. This experiment has since been followed up in the treatment of a wide range of disorders, asthma, coughs, headaches, post-operative pain, sea sickness, and many more. The results have been surprisingly constant: between a half and a third of all patients are placebo-reactors.

The term "placebo" ordinarily refers to a pill made out of some substance which is pharmacologically inert, or to coloured water. But even water can cause a physical or chemical reaction, in certain circumstances; so sometimes—to quote Dr. J. B. Harman, in his recent article on the subject in the *Prescribers Journal*—"a respected drug that is pharmacologically effective in other circumstances" may be used as a placebo—aspirin, is by far the most widely employed.

There can be placebo treatments of other kinds. Some orthopedic surgeons are convinced that where osteopaths succeed, it is not by manipulating the patient's spinal column, but by bending his mind. There have even been placebo operations—though the fact is not generally recognised until they have ceased to be practised: treating "focal sepsis", for example, by the removal of all a patient's teeth.

But whatever the technique, the point is that placebo-effect is an astonishingly potent therapeutic force, whose full range of performance is only just beginning to be appreciated. For example, it has been found that placeboes do not necessarily assist the therapeutic process; they can be used to inhibit it, or even baffle it. Steward Wolf, the American researcher who has done more than anybody else to illuminate the subject, once gave a woman an emetic, assuring her it was a treatment for her vomiting. Not merely did it stop her being sick; her stomach juices actually reacted as if it were an anti-emetic.

But why, if it has produced such remarkable results, have the merits of this wonder drug not been more widely sung?

Well, there is the unfortunate but undeniable complication that the effect of placeboes is limited by the fact that as soon as a patient realises he is getting them, they cease to work. It may even be that the 30-50 per cent success rate over the past few years will drop simply because the public is becoming aware how extensively placeboes are being used.

A doctor, too, may understandably be a little chary of using placeboes, even when he is convinced they will work, in case he should be found out. If his patients discover they are being given dummy pills they are apt to be indignant; they might even sue.

Yet I do not believe that these are the real reasons for the profession's lack of confidence in placebo-effect as a therapeutic aid. The fact is that it happens to be inconvenient, because it constitutes indisputable proof of the reality of faith healing. And to ask the profession to accept the existence of faith healing has been like asking the Vatican to accept Dr. Allegro's version of the origins of Christianity.

I know of only one form of placebo treatment, which the medical profession has adopted as a recognised, if not yet standard, technique; its use in getting rid of children's warts. Many general practitioners, and not a few consultants, will now tell parents to use folk remedies. The application of dandelion juice, in England— or the practice of "buying" the wart (sixpence used to be the usual fee) in Ireland—are accepted as quicker and cheaper remedies than cauterisation.

But this method, too, has crept in under the euphemism "suggestion"; it is not described as placebo therapy. The placebo, in fact, has had to achieve respectability by a very different route: as an adjunct in the trials of new drugs.

The method now commonly used when a new drug is being tested is to divide the patients to be tested into two groups; one getting the drug, the other—the control group—getting the placebo. The experiment then proceeds "double blind", neither patients nor medical staff knowing which patients are getting the placebo, and which the drug. And half way through the trials, in case a majority of the placebo-reactors should by mischance be bunched in one of the groups, there is a "cross over", so that those who have been on the drug switch to the placebo, and *vice versa*.

The results of trials using this system have often been chastening, cutting wonder drugs down to size. The classic example was the test of the tranquilliser meprobamate, sold here under the brand names Miltown and Equanil. It had been one of the most profitable drugs ever marketed—but in the trials, the placebo proved just as effective

"There's nothing really wrong with me, Doctor—I just thought I'd drop in to see if you've come up with any new diets."

(meprobamate was eventually taken out of the US *Pharmacopoeia*—the pharmaceutical equivalent of a doctor being struck off the register).

Again and again, the placebo has repeated this remarkable performance when pitted against other tranquillisers, anti-depressants, cures for smoking, and drugs used in the treatment of rheumatic disorders—indomethacin (Indocid), for one. This has been extensively promoted for rheumatoid arthritis sufferers, and has made a fortune for Merck's shareholders; yet trials both here and in the US have shown that a placebo performs just as successfully.

When I drew attention to the results of these trials in an article, I got indignant letters from patients to say that I must be wrong, as after years of martyrdom to rheumatoid arthritis, Indocid had been prescribed, and had cured or greatly relieved them. And it was no use writing back to say I did not doubt them: that my point was simply that the cure, or relief, might have equally well been obtained by placebo effect (and perhaps *was*, for all they knew). The fact is that most of us are still proud to have been cured by a drug, yet feel humiliated at the idea that we may have been cured by placebo-effect.

But why should we feel embarrassment? To be able to cure ourselves by an effort of the imagination (albeit unconscious) is an achievement: it shows that our built-in protective mechanism is in good working order. And how much better that it should be, than that we should have to rely on expensive drugs, with their often unpleasant side reactions! When this is realised, the discovery of placebo-effect will be remembered as one of the great contributions to medicine of our era, along with antibiotics—and possibly long after antibiotics have been superseded.

But this prompts the question: how does placebo-effect work? Is it simply a matter of auto-suggestion, or can it be induced—like hypnosis—by the doctor?

The way belief in a drug may influence its effectiveness was recalled not long ago in a leading article in the *British Medical Journal*. A doctor with an intractable case of asthma on his hands used to try out each new drug advertised for the disorder, and eventually he found one to which the patient reacted very favourably. To be on the safe side, the doctor tried him with a placebo; it did not work. Convinced that he was on to a winner, the doctor ordered a supply of the new drug. The firm replied, in some embarrassment, that there had been a mistake, the "new drug" which they had sent him had, in fact, been placebo tablets . . .

Since then, there have been other interesting pointers. A few years ago, for example, a controlled trial, double blind, was done on a new anti-depressant. Half the patients were given pills from container A, half from container B, but nobody knew which container held the drug, and which the placebo. However, it early on became apparent that patients on "A" were doing better than those on "B" and naturally this aroused hopes that "A" was the drug and that it was proving effective.

The real test came with the cross-over: would the patients who had been on "B" do better when they switched to "A"? And sure enough, they did. So here was a drug which had broken the barrier!

Or so it seemed. But no; for after the trials were finished, it was disclosed that there had been no cross-over at the half way stage after all—only a pretence of one. There were only two possible explanations for what had happened. Either the members of the staff, coming to believe that container A held the drug, had later deceived themselves into thinking that patients on A were doing better; or, their confidence in the A had some way seeped through to the patients, so that they actually *were* better—not because of the drug, but because of the confidence.

The most likely explanation is that the doctor/patient relationship can have a marked effect on the results of treatment—and this has in fact been shown by Wolf, in a simple experiment. He divided patients with stomach trouble into two matched groups, both of which were given the same placebo treatment; the only difference being that one group got their placeboes from Dr. Y, the other from Dr. Z. Dr. Y's patients showed a twelve per cent increase in gastric acidity: Dr. Z's an eighteen per cent decrease.

But we do not know why this happens, or how it happens, (to say "through suggestion" gets us little further: *why? how?*) All we know for certain is that placebo-effect can and does produce surprising, and occasionally spectacular, results. And at least these have solved a couple of long-standing medical mysteries. One was enshrined in the old medical tag, "use your new drugs quickly, while they still have the power to cure"; and the other mystery that the research into placebo-effect has helped solve is why most of us react more favourably to one particular brand of, say, aspirin than to others, though pharmacologically they may be indistinguishable. It may be the ads—or simply the colour, size or shape of the pill—but whatever it is, it is simply placebo-effect, working on us, that makes it *our* drug.

And of course this applies to a vast range of remedies, some of them used since civilisation began. There are, for example, innumerable jujus to ward off rheumatism, from herbs to copper bangles. They may have no scientific justification, in the sense that there is no reason to suppose that they have any direct physical or chemical influence; yet indirectly they may work, and work very powerfully, through placebo-effect.

That this should be so is, admittedly, something of an embarrassment. As Dr. S. Bradshaw showed in his admirable survey, *The Drugs You Take*, a prodigious amount is spent annually on off-prescription medicaments which can be shown to be pharmacologically worthless—and sometimes harmful, as in the case of purgatives to keep the taker "regular". Even when they are harmless, there is something irritating about seeing so much of the national income spent in this way, particularly as the taxpayer has to provide part of the cost through the NHS. But this is less an argument for seeking ways to prevent people from that form of spending, than for more extensive research into whatever it is that makes these nostrums work—in other words, research into placebo-effect.

"Now, if I hurt you, just let out an agonized shriek."

... and as if that weren't enough, the doctors also have to contend with that Patients' Association report of callousness and unconcern by GPs. LARRY went down to his local surgery to check the story out . . .

Visitors to Britain!
Why Not Try Our Exciting Tour 101a—
The Tour Which Really Gets Inside
The British

Cruise passengers from the QE2 visited hospitals in Canton and watched operations in progress—one of them on a female patient anaesthetised by acupuncture

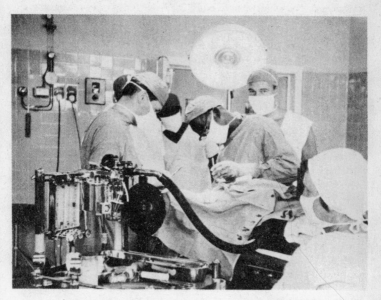

Just one of the spectacular outings laid on by your courier

DAY ONE
  0530 Arrive Heathrow Airport. Coach to Claridges Hotel.

  1000-1015 Optional Visit to British Museum.

  1030-1130 "Fishbones and Wishbones"—a morning of simple gullet extractions at St. Lupus's Throat Hospital.

  1130-1215 Blood donations by group, followed by cup of hot, sweet tea.

  1230 Luncheon at St. Lupus's Out-Patients Canteen.

  1400-1415 Tour of an infectious diseases hospital.

  1445-1515 At leisure in Carnaby Street.

  1530-1645 Tour of another infectious diseases hospital.

  1900 Gala Dinner at Claridges.

DAY TWO

1000-1015 Optional Tour of National Gallery.

1030-1230 "How The British Tick"—a number of patients chosen at random at King William Hospital for Senior Officers will be opened up to display their curious workings. The circulation of blue blood is a unique attraction.

Those who do not wish to witness operations may remain in the Out-Patients Canteen.

If, on account of industrial action, no operations are being performed, there will be a special screening of "Dracula: The Feast of Blood" in No. 1 Operating Theatre.

1400-1630 "Harley Street, Artery of Romance". The Golden Mile of Rolls-Royces. The quiet waiting-rooms where rare germs are exchanged. The unmistakable, haunting drone rising from a thousand psychiatrists' couches. Medical hypnotists and artificial inseminationists beckon from the windows. A husky-voiced otorhinolaryngologist talks of life, death and VAT.

2000-2100 Visit to a Lock Hospital, with lantern lecture on "The Dangers of Ignorance".

2100-2330 At leisure in Soho.

DAY THREE

0500 FFI (Freedom From Infection) Examination.

0530-0945 Coach to Stratford-upon-Avon.

1000-1230 Visits to selected National Health doctors' surgeries, with opportunities to palpate the patients.

1400-1420 Sightseeing in historic Stratford, a town with many clinics and hospitals.

1500-1630 Alcoholics Anonymous Group Therapy Session at St. Jeremiah's Hospital, Stratford. All alcoholic members of the group will be expected to participate.

1700-2000 Coach to London.

2200-2350 Late, Late Show in a leading geriatric ward, with problem Cockney patients.

DAY FOUR

The entire day is spent in a private hospital for patients from the Middle East, watching the newest methods of monetary transfusion and rejuvenation of bank accounts. A simple six-course luncheon is included, wine extra.

DAY FIVE

0900-1200 Demonstrations by members of National Union of Public Employees at Queen Anne's Samaritan Hospital of discriminatory feeding techniques applied to patients. How native Britons are prevented from "buying health".

1230 Luncheon prepared by NUPE, followed by luncheon at Claridges.

1400-1420 Chamber of Horrors, Madame Tussaud's.

1445-1600 Museum of Horrors, Royal College of Surgeons.

DAY SIX

0900-1230 "London, the Abortion Capital of the World". Split into small groups, we "follow the crowd" from Heathrow and learn what goes on in the modern Temples of Aesculapius. A talk on job satisfaction by a leading surgeon.

1400-2330 National Film Theatre: *The Rest of Dr. Finlay's Casebook*.

DAY SEVEN

Request Day. If you wish to visit a family planning clinic, a criminal lunatic asylum, an emergency ward full of motor-cyclists or even an ear, elbow and toe hospital, state your choice before 0800.

1600-1700 Blood donations by all members of group.

2200-2345 Late Night Extra—only for the strong! Six midwives describe their most difficult cases.

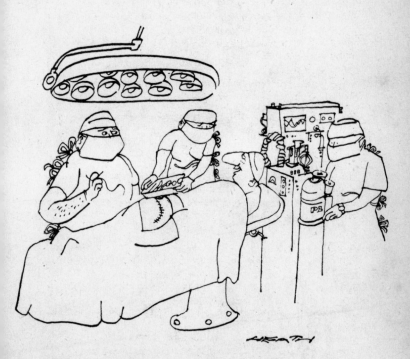

"Have I told you about my operation?"

Hospital Splendide

HEATH on converting hotels
for private medicine

"I can't find your name—are you sure you booked?"

Mr. and Mrs. Smith."

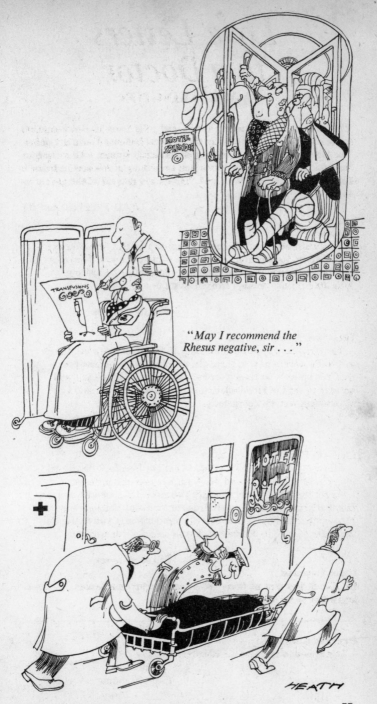

"*May I recommend the Rhesus negative, sir . . .*"

HEATH

Love Letters
to a Doctor
by MILES KINGTON

"A 'passion file' containing letters and gifts from love-sick patients
to their doctors is being kept by the Medical Defence Union in London.
The letters are mainly written by middle-class women with a crush on
their doctors . . . 'When a doctor gets something of this sort he treats it
like a hot potato,' Dr. Wall said. 'He always gets rid of the patient on
to someone else's list' . . ."

(*DAILY TELEGRAPH*).

Dear Dr. Grant,
  You must help me. I can hardly sleep at nights. I lie awake in a
sort of fever, tossing and turning, just thinking of you. I have lost my
appetite and seem no longer able to concentrate on anything.
You are the only person I can tell about this.
> yours
> Elizabeth Jones

Dear Mrs. Jones,
  I am transferring you immediately to Dr. Horslock's list. I hope
you will understand that there can never be anything between us and
that it is better if we do not see each other again. I trust you will
recover soon; Dr. Horslock is an excellent practitioner and I
recommend her wholeheartedly.
> yours sincerely
> Arthur Grant

Dear Dr. Grant,
  I thought you might like to know that Dr. Horslock diagnosed
my trouble as influenza and that I am now in excellent health.
  As for the other matter to which you refer, I had no idea you felt
like that about me and I can only admire the way you have always
hidden these feelings. It was entirely honourable of you to transfer
me to Dr. Horslock. Rest assured your secret is safe with me.
> yours
> Elizabeth Jones

Union Comment
**Dr. Grant has sent us thirty other similar correspondences. We have
urged him to be less suspicious.**

Dear Dr. Anstruther,
  I want you to examine me all over.
> yours
> Fiona Standing

Dear Mrs. Standing,
   How do you mean?

Dr. Anstruther

Dear Dr. Anstruther,
   What I say. I want you to take a look at my body. Please.

yours
Fiona Standing

Dear Mrs. Standing,
   Yes, but is there any particular reason? I mean, what do you have in mind? I would appreciate a detailed answer before I can make an appointment.

yours
Dr. Anstruther

Dear Dr. Anstruther,
   Yes, there is something special I want you to see.

yours
Fiona Standing

Dear Mrs. Standing,
   I hope you will understand if I tell you there is now a special questionnaire I am sending to female patients who wish to be examined. Please fill it in and return.
   1. What are your feelings about your doctor?
   2. Do you undertake to behave as I ask you during any physical examination?
   3. Are you happily married?
   4. If necessary, would you consent to have someone else present during the examination?

yours
Dr. Anstruther

Dear Dr. Anstruther,
   I find your veiled proposals nauseating. If I cannot request my doctor for a straightforward chest check-up without being invited to an orgy, whom can one trust? Thank God I found out in time.

yours
Fiona Standing

Union Comment
Mrs. Standing was transferred to Dr. Horslock's list, at her own request.

To Dr. Carstairs
My darling,
   I cannot wait to see you again. I love you so terribly it hurts. I think of you night and day. But it won't be long now.

all my love
Kate

Union Comment
Dr. Carstairs has requested the return of this letter, which he now realises is from his wife.

Dear Dr. Hastings,

I have been recommended to come to you for treatment of my complaint. Briefly, my symptoms are that I blush very easily, twist my hands, stammer, cry without warning and tend to swoon.
I would like to see you as soon as possible.

yours sincerely
Virginia Maltby (Mrs.)

Dear Mrs. Maltby,

Before I make an appointment to study your ailment, it would help me to know who had recommended you to me for treatment.

yours sincerely
Dr. Hastings

Dear Dr. Hastings,

I have been passed on to you by, in chronological order,
Drs. Grant, Anstruther, Campbell, Woodleigh, Simpson (père et fils), Hay, Mendoza, Wilcox, Bentinck and Carstairs.

Virginia Maltby (Mrs.)

Dear Mrs. Maltby,

I am referring you to a Dr. Horslock, who will probably be able to help you more than I can.

yours sincerely
Dr. Hastings

Union Comment
Thank God for Horslock.

Dear Dr. Woodleigh,

Just a hasty note to tell you that I have eaten too many oysters and fear this has led to my present strange condition. May I come and see you?

yours
Margaret Price

Dear Mrs. Price,

It is, ah, possible that oysters may, as it were, have an effect on you, but I would not worry. Why not pop in, in, well, a few weeks' time and let me see. But meanwhile *for God's sake* don't take any more oysters, or shellfish, or rhino horn, or Spanish fly, or champagne, or lampreys Promise? If you don't feel any better meanwhile, I'd get in touch with Dr. Horslock, who's very good on these things.

yours
Dr. Woodleigh, er, Jim

Union Comment
Surprised he didn't warn her off love filtres.

Dear Dr. Hay,

Just a note to say thank you for the pills, which did the trick. Really, to be honest, I wanted to know how *you* were feeling. I couldn't help noticing, when I came in for my check-up, that you were obviously under the weather. I mean, the way you were sweating, and hid hunched up behind your desk, and retreated with a great start every time I came near you—it seems obvious to me you've been overworking and that you won't admit you're ill. Is it something to do with your eyes? I say that because, between you and me, I *did* notice that when you were examining me you actually had your eyes fixed on the far end of the room. I told Jim about it (in all secrecy) and he's worried about it too. You must look after yourself. Love to Sarah.

yours
Betty Pike

Union Comment
Man's a fool.

Dear Dr. Mendoza,

Nothing personal, but I am getting a bit tired of your examinations. For the last few years you have only viewed me through binoculars from the far end of your surgery. I would understand if I were highly infectious, but even that would not explain the dark glasses, the trilby pulled down over the forehead and the loaded gun on the desk. Can you please recommend me another practitioner?

yours
Violet Ponsonby

Dear Lady Ponsonby,
   Dr. Horslock.

yours
X

Union Comment
Hmm.

Dear Dr. Horslock,
   I love you.

yours
Desperate

Dear Desperate,
   There's a lot of it going around. Have you tried aspirin?

yours
Sensible

Union Comment
God give us more Horslocks.

Doctor v. Patient

"Keep getting this recurrent nightmare where all my 3,000 panel go sick together . . . "

"And what might your views be on GPs' pay and conditions?"

*"What's up then? Reading room full, pubs closed,
nothing on the telly?"*

"My mind's made up, Henry—either you go ex-directory or I quit."

83

Doctor on the S

*Seventy London hospitals and medical schools are being linked by
is being planned soberly enough; but once it gets going th*

Next Patient, Please

There is likely to be a large audience for
the new round of *Clinical Quiz*, which
kicks off next week with Bart's v The
Society of Apothecaries. Cases are being
groomed to provide some really tough
problems in diagnosis. However, we
shan't be seeing the legendary Mrs. B,
who became the star of last season with
her ability to produce a rash by willpower.

He's a TV Doctor Now!

The one-time Radio Doctor is taking time
off from chairing the BBC to introduce
Sportsnight With Hill. The next edition
will include the Suture-Relay Race from
the Army Medical School and the replay
of the Tonsillectomy Handicap.

The Crystal Ball

Who will be the next President of the
Royal College of Surgeons? This is only
one of the topics for discussion by the
panel in *Doctor's Dilemma*, which comes
this week from Walthamstow Foot Clinic.
There is one new member of the team,
pretty Sister Samantha Phlox from the
London Senile Dementia Classifying
Centre. As usual, Jimmy Savile will be in
the chair to represent the layman's point
of view.

Perilous Post-mortem

A knotty puzzle faces *Brent Hawleigh* this
week and his investigations lead him into
serious danger. The handsome path-
ologist has nothing to go on but two left
hands. The guest expert in this episode is
the Director of the Sheffield Flying
Dissection Squad.

Chop Chop

The visit of the Chinese medical troupe
was a chance not to be missed and they
were soon persuaded to appear on tele-

vision. Viewers will be able to see them
action, as the whole of this mont
Surgical Novelties is being given up t
display of their dazzling technique. Wa
out for the Chung Brothers' work with
two-handed saw and the demonstrati
of mass acupuncture.

What's He Got?

Open Line has soon established itself
the affection of the public. This is
programme where the diagnosticians
the studio are rung up *on the set* by G
with problem cases. Using the local m

TOMORROW'S H
Any Volunteers? *From the*

ren

circuit TV. At first Channel 7
for ratings will begin.

...heir eyes and ears, they try to identify
...condition. It's the clash of views that
...kes the drama. The team have never
...eed on a diagnosis up to now.
...donic Professor Emrys Macphail will
...in be in charge. His, "Well, ask him,
...n" has become quite a catch-phrase.

...ulletin

...ry Parkley's many well-wishers will be
...d to know that he is as well as can be
...ected after the accident he sustained
...le acting as Commentator for the
...ctical of the FRCS examination.

...HT' 8.15.
...Iall Abbot's Fibula.

Sun.

8.30 am	**Morning Service.** Massed choirs and sermon from the Neuralgia Ward, St. Mary's.
9-12 am	**Keep Up to Date.** Appendix Transplant Part 1.
3 pm	**Annals of Anatomy.** 14. Prior Gyrth and the Discovery of the Patella.
4-7 pm	Appendix Transplant Part 2.

Tues.

7.30 am	**First Aid for Doctors.**
3 pm	**New Substitutes For Oxygen.**
8.15 pm	**Invalid Diet.** Fanny Cradock. This week: Some interesting Gruel recipes from the Dodecanese.

Fri.

8 pm	**The Royal Physicians.** Live debate from the London Hospital Union, with Richard Crossman, Godfrey Winn.
11 pm	**Late Night Cabaret.** Smoking Concert from the Royal Free.

Sat.

11.30 am	Appendix Transplant: final stages.
2 pm (approx.)	**Ca Vous Fait Mal, Hein?** This week Peter and Pam try to explain to Dr. Mouchard that while bathing she has been bitten by a labrador.
5 pm	**The Child Psychologist:** Siamese Twins.
10 pm	**Open Forum.** Neurogynaecology and the Permissive Society.

A PATIENT'S
CASEBOOK

By DAVID STONE

I MADE a neat list of my ailments the other morning and after studying them for a few minutes I decided that they justified a visit to my doctor.

I don't like him very much because his opening words as I limp trembling into his consulting room are inevitably: "Goodness, you're looking well today." This always has the effect of making me feel like Charles Atlas, and the symptoms which had been of such consuming interest to future readers of the *Lancet* die unspoken on my lips.

However this morning was a different matter. No one of such worth to the medical profession as I am should walk the streets unaided, and I dialled his number.

The receptionist's soothing voice took on a jagged note when she heard my name.

"The doctor's very busy today. You always like a long time, don't you?"

"Me?" I said indignantly. "Goodness no. I just wanted a few words with him."

"Yes," she said, "all right then. I suppose you couldn't make a quarter to three?"

"On the dot," I replied.

There was a pause, and then she said that would be all right.

As I rang his bell, I suddenly realized I'd forgotten what it was—what they were, rather—that ailed me, but I still managed a brave smile for the receptionist. She stared at me in the way I imagine the man who'd gone to Cape Canaveral to get away from it all looked when they told him the news.

On the short walk between the waiting room and his consulting room I became once more a human medical casebook, one of those miracles of survival the newspapers always print pictures of. Shooting pains, imaginary fears, obscure aches, a general feeling of malaise, all were mine, but substantiated by good prosaic stuff as well.

My doctor was not, as he usually is on my visits, standing in front of a Peter Scott lithograph of duck flighting, filling his curly pipe with rich, masculine smelling tobacco.

I thought I was alone in the room at first, and I was just about to have a go with the sphygmometer when there was a sort of sigh from the corner.

My doctor was sitting on the edge of his couch, staring at me in a listless way.

"Hello," I said.

"Ah," he paused, "now, what was it?"

"Well . . ." I wondered whether to start with the loss of the use of my limbs in the automatic lift when I pressed the ASCEND button, or the feelings of unreality that overtook me when both the telephones on my desk rang at the same time. Then I looked at my doctor again.

"How are *you*?" I said.

"Oh, I don't know," he said, staring at the bound copies of the *Practitioner* in the bookcase. "I seem to feel permanently tired these days."

"What do you mean?"

"Oh, I get up, work, go to bed; everything seems meaningless."

"Perhaps you should get a hobby," I said.

"I haven't even got the energy for that," he replied. "Everything seems a strain. I don't enjoy life any more. I keep asking myself what it all means."

"Do you sleep all right?" I asked.

"No, very badly. I just lie there thinking."

"What about?"

"Oh, the futility of temporal ambition," he said. "I have this constant feeling that I'm not doing the right thing, and yet I'm trapped by circumstances. What I'd really love to do is just live in a cottage in Galway and fish all day long."

"Have you any idea what's behind this?" I asked.

He raised his sad eyes to mine.

"It's making decisions all day long. That's all my job is. Making decisions. I can't stand it any longer."

"You know what's the matter with you?" I said.

"What?"

"You need a holiday. Everyone has these feelings when they've been working too hard. I promise you, go on holiday and you'll feel right as rain."

My doctor smiled for the first time that afternoon.

"Do you really think so?" he said. I said I was sure of it, and my last words, as I said goodbye to him at the front door, were:

"Don't forget now, get right away from it all."

As it happened I found myself in a night club in the small hours of the following morning, and I was very surprised to see my doctor on the dance floor. The dim, red-shaded lights made him look as though he was bursting with health, and he was dancing a tremendously gay cha-cha-cha with a lady I wasn't sure the BMA would wholly approve of.

As I watched him do a particularly fancy hip-swing I reflected that anyone who didn't know him would have put my doctor down as a man who was relaxing heartily after a hard day ministering to the needs of the sick and neurotic instead of a broken reed. It gave me quite a lot to think about.

Food for Fears

By R. G. G. PRICE

I AM a hypochondriac: I imagine I have all sorts of diseases although I don't do much about preventing them. Not for me the wool next the skin, the protein-free diet, the press-ups. I have a vivid imagination and a magpie memory for overheard fragments of medical conversation; but I find it difficult to get a good supply of the raw material on which we night-tremblers feed. Medical textbooks are expensive if new and too soothing secondhand, when many of the ailments they describe may have been stamped out. I feel embarrassed disease-hunting in Public Libraries and unfortunately the medical literature on my own shelves provides pretty patchy coverage.

First Aid manuals seem somehow nearer to surgery than to medicine. I doubt whether any hypochondriac gets himself into a state by imagining he has a fractured clavicle or is suffering from varicose veins or poisoning by corrosives. My wife inherited a *Woman's Home Doctor* and this has provided me with a certain amount of raw material for my fears. The trouble is that it is slanted. It is full of warnings that in this or that condition it is essential that the husband should be forbearing with his wife. There is nothing about a woman's duties towards a man who is seized with violent pains that, according to the labels on the shingled nude in the frontispiece, should mean trouble in the womb.

Mere rules of health are no use to the man who is getting a bit bored with imagining that flu is coming on, so Dr. Parkes's little book on *Personal Care of Health*, which had reached 38,000 by 1887, is not much help. It says things like that the hair should be kept clean or else "it forms a harbour for plants" but this does not provide me with any new disease. I find it possible to visualise and fear. Similarly a lurid-looking book on *Intoxicating Drinks—Their History and Mystery* (by the author of *Buy Your Own Cherries*) tells me that a doctor in Brussels proved that absinthe works faster than prussic acid but does not supply me with symptoms. The *Ladies' New Dispensatory* of 1769 is slightly better. Relaxation of the Uvula, for example, is a fresh idea to me. (The cure is either a gargle, that includes pomegranate peel and balaustines or stroking up the hair of the head for some time with a little brandy and ointment of marshmallows. Well, that is what it says. After all, the recipe for heartburn does include an ounce of powdered crab's eyes.) On nervous disorders the writer says they can be moderated by serenity of mind. This is about as helpful as *Beauty Through Hygiene*, which says bleakly that girls who are devoted to society are almost invariably poor breathers. So much for the random bookshelf.

Old hypochondriacs used to get inspiration from the medical bulletins on the eminent. Some duke would be reported as sinking and they would feel they were sinking too. Today bulletins are usually rather vague. "Has entered hospital for a minor operation" is a stock phrase. The best I have done on this foundation is a scare in which I imagined going in for a minor operation, which I visualised as an ingrowing toenail, and the surgeon going mad and not stopping. Another obvious source of material is one's friends; but owing to some deficiency of perception I never seem to realise that people have been ill until I meet them well again and no hypochondriac can get much benefit from conversation with a man who says "My doctor got me on my feet again in no time."

It is this inefficiency of technical intake that is responsible, I think, for making so many of my night fears peculiar to myself. My diseases are not shared; they are evolved from my inner consciousness. There is a shooting pain from my left heel to my abdomen, for example. This, I decide, is due to deficiency in my diet. Unfortunately my chemistry at school hardly got beyond the chemistry-box stage and therefore the kind of things my diet tends to lack are copper sulphate, zinc and potassium chlorate. The spasmodic contraction of my diaphragm is due to caries of the spleen: it needs fillings. The curious sensation as though some large, cold, wet sea-creature were nuzzling my spine is Imperfect Adjustment to Temperature Changes leading to reversed sweating and, eventually, to neural erosion. The feeling that my heart is slowly swinging round at its moorings is the inevitable concomitant of cardiac palsy.

I have often thought of becoming a medical student, not for all the breezy nurse-slapping and beer-drinking and certainly not with any intention of passing exams—I am much too interested in my own ills to wish to treat other people's—but simply to restock my limited repertoire of alarms. On the whole, however, I think my best source of gruesome suggestions, of fine wrought fears, of ingenious tremors, is simply to lie and imagine I am a patient of the hospital Dr. Richard Gordon writes about.

"*You make it seem such fun, Walter. I sometimes think I wouldn't mind being a hypochondriac!*"

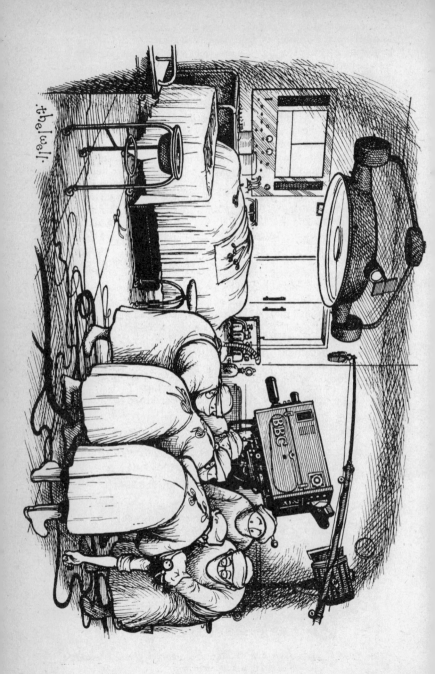

A Vision in Harley Street

IN Harley Street, one foggy night and raw,
I swear by Æsculapius I saw
For one tense second in the swirling mist
An otorhinolaryngologist.

A memorable night it was for me,
Though other men conceivably may be
Well used to slapping guineas in the fists
Of otorhinolaryngologists.

As one in fealty to the National Health,
I hope it isn't true that private wealth
Alone empowers a patient to enlist
An otorhinolaryngologist.

I wonder if their rooms are brown and solemn,
With Harvey's bust upon a fluted column?
How human are they? Has a woman kissed
An otorhinolaryngologist?

Long years ago I knew a Dr. Groat,
A splendid man for ears and nose and throat;
He never dreamed that one day would exist
An otorhinolaryngologist.

I must go down to Harley Street once more . . .
Though probably it won't be long before
One half of its nine hundred specialists
Are otorhinolaryngologists.

E. S. TURNER

Many patients feel doctors overcharge. Many doctors share that view but it is only the patients who get sore about it.

The current vogue among doctors is "Group practice." If collective medical effort fails, they croon "Rock of Ages" in spread harmony as you go.

American doctors no longer "push and probe" but rely on scientific tests instead. However, an exception will be made in the case of the patient entering the ante-room and the doctor will "push and probe" until he feels much better.

While patients devote all their energies to illness, doctors are in short supply and are very overworked.

In Sickness
and in Health

ALAN COREN

IT was just the other day—July 10, 1984, to be exact—that I found
myself limping through the august portico of the Royal Free
Thomtholomew's College Hospital, London's wonderful National
Health co-operative, in the hope of finding a soothing hand to bind
up an ankle sprained the previous night in a nasty gin accident.

The casualty department was, as we who are fortunate enough to
live upon this happy island have long come to expect, a model of
efficiency: the injured had been neatly sorted into piles, each patient
carefully labelled with his date of entry and next-of-kin, the poly-
thene bags of dead hung on clever little pegs convenient to the
garbage disposal, the Muzak had thoughtfully been turned up to
drown the shrieks of the inconsiderate maimed, and the bright red
carpet upon the floor had been brilliantly chosen so that colour
took its correct priority over sterility.

I could not have been sitting there for more than a day or so when
an attractive young boilerman came along, examined the number
stencilled on my forehead, blew his nose on his apron and said:

"The Chief Shop Steward will see you now."

Carefully stepping over two of my recent neighbours, a pair of
road accident victims betrayed by weak-willed impatience into
attempting to amputate one another's legs, I followed the nurse
down a long dark corridor, no easy journey, given the difficulty of
beating flies off while hopping on one leg, and found myself, at last,
being shown into a comfortable consulting room that bore all the
familiar hallmarks of senior medical occupancy: an elegant *Penthouse*
calendar, a worn dartboard, a Bass dispenser, and an up-ended
packing case at which four men in dungarees and rubber gloves were
playing brag.

"Who's this, then?" said the tallest of the four. "Your two quid,
and up two."

"786544," said the boilerman. "He's got a hobble."

"Oh, has he?" said the Chief Shop Steward. "I'll see you for a
fiver."

"But I thought it was free here?" I said.

"You speak when you're bleeding spoke to!" snapped the Chief
Shop Steward. "I'm talking to *him*. Christ Almighty, three fours!
Werl, that's me out, you lot better get off and start operating." He
threw his cards down and turned to me. "All right, take your clothes
off, have you brought a thermometer?"

"I really don't see that that's necessary, Doctor, all I wanted
was . . ."

The Chief Shop Steward narrowed his little eyes.

*"If you don't like the treatment
you are getting you can always
be sick to rule or withdraw
your ailment!"*

"You watch who you're calling doctor, son!" he barked. "I happen to be CSS of NUPE, Head of this great hospital, also one of the country's leading caretakers! Some people," and here he prodded my chest with such authority that I was forced to hop suddenly backwards, "do not realise what it takes to be a great caretaker, son. The years of training, the terrible hours, all them mops to see to."

"Forgive me," I said, "I didn't realise to whom I was speaking. It's just a sprain, a doctor would be perfectly adequate, I don't know why they bothered you, sir, I . . ."

"Everybody has to come through me," said the CSS. "Unless I'm certain it's a genuine bona fide case, they're out of here so fast their feet don't touch the ground! Or in your case, foot. Take your sock off, I'll get a quack sent up."

He strode to the door, threw it open, shouted "QUACK!" into the echoing gloom, and within half a minute we were rewarded with the clatter of scuttling boots, closely followed by a small panting man entirely wrapped in mangy fur, through the top of which his saffron face was peeking. He bowed to the CSS.

"Bugger me," said the Head of the hospital, "it would be bloody him!"

The doctor laughed, and rocked back and forth.

"He's a Lapp," said the CSS. "Can't speak a word of English. Some of our quacks have got a word or two, know what I mean, but your eskimo is a slow sod. Except when it comes to ears. He can't half take off ears, this one."

"How is he," I said, "on sprained ankles?"

"Oh, he never touches legs. He's an ear, nose and throat man. And bloody deft. You ought to see him skin a seal."

The doctor plucked at my sleeve, nodding his head towards the door.

"Tell him about my ankle!" I cried, somewhat urgently.

"Can't tell him nothing," said the CSS. "He'll do a marvellous job on your ears, though. Tomorrow morning, you'll never know you ever had 'em. He even fills in the holes. You're a lucky lad."

"But there's nothing wrong with my ears!" I shouted.

"I'll be the best judge of that, mate! There's always something wrong with ears, fiddling bloody things, all them corners, real dirt traps. If I let you go away now, you mark my words you'll be back here one day, going on about earache and so forth, you have 'em off while you got the chance, son! You don't realise how lucky you are, he clocks off in half an hour, any later and you'd have had Doctor Ching, he removes kidneys by acupuncture, or tries to."

I shook myself free of the Lapp, who snarled a little, but settled.

"Have you no English doctors here?" I cried.

The Chief Shop Steward stared at me.

"When was you last in a hospital?" he said.

"Oh, it must be, what? Ten, twelve years ago. Early 1970s."

"*Ten years?* Bloody dark ages, son! Bloody oppressive yolk of Victorian wossname! Oh, they had English doctors, *then*, all right, poncing about in their three-piece whistles and laying down the law, taking organs out, sewing up people, sticking needles in all and sundry on their own initiative, no reference to cleaning staff, not a word to the car-park attendants, walking into operating theatres big as you please and up to their elbows in someone's innards without even a by-your-leave to the girls on the switchboard, you'd have thought it was Nazi bleeding Germany! Well, we couldn't have that, could we? We couldn't have democracy made a nonsense of and stand idly by, right?"

"I suppose not," I said.

"A lot of our members was for hanging 'em outright, werl, there's always the odd extremist, know what I mean, but the voice of moderation was heard in the land, brother. Just scrap the private sector, we said, that'll have 'em running off to America and Sweden and Holland and Australia and all them other places still suffering beneath the tyrannical heel of the quack, with a bit of luck it'll all be over by Christmas. 'Course, we were prepared to let some of the younger ones stay on, some of those on two-and-a-half grand for a hundred-hour week, nobody minded as long as they were making less than the cooks etcetera, also not interfering in the running of the hospitals, but they're a militant lot, your doctors, not to mention greedy and grasping, always on about more pay, no thought for the welfare of the country, know what I mean, self before state, it's what comes of not growing up in a trade union tradition, am I right?"

"Absolutely," I said.

"So they left. Proved our point. If you want to get rid of private medicine what's occupying a monstrous almost five per cent of the industry, eroding democracy as we know it, robbing the individual of the right to choose to be indistinguishable from anyone else, making a farce of all that we have decided to call freedom, then it's no good mucking about with shutting a ward here, bringing a hospital to its knees there. If you want to get rid of private medicine, you have to go right to the root cause, right?"

"You have to get rid of the doctors?"

"Exactly! I can see you're not slow, son. Pity about that, I've got a nice position as brain surgeon going for a willing illiterate. Anyhow, after the English quacks all cleared off, we started attracting the right sort of people. You know, vets, pelmanists, masseurs, plumbers, and they tided us over until the foreign failures started to catch on to the wonderful opportunities. Like Nanook here, or whatever his name is, always wanted to be a doctor, so we put him through medical school, full six months course, and he's so grateful he'll do anything we tell him, as long as it's ears."

"Ears!" shouted the surgeon, "Ears!"

"Only word he knows," said the Chief Shop Steward. He patted his head. "You little treasure!" he said. "Never have any trouble with him, never interferes, leaves the running of the hospital to them as knows about it, don't you, Nanook?"

"Ears!"

"You'll have to go with him, son," said the Chief Shop Steward. "He can turn very nasty if he thinks an ear's getting away."

"But . . ."

"Don't argue, son, he'll have a scalpel in you soon as look at you, this one."

I turned, and hobbled out. Half way up the corridor, the Chief Shop Steward's voice boomed after me.

"You ought to get that leg of yours seen to, son," he called. "It won't get better on its own!"

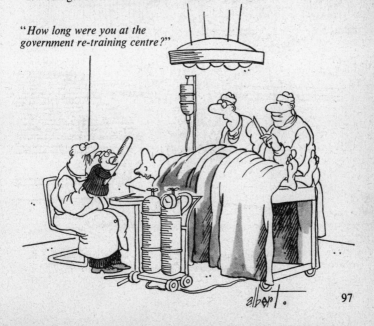

"*How long were you at the government re-training centre?*"

97

"*I want one with a thinly-veiled accusation of malingering.*"

"*Surely you must have something more suitable for an ailing clergyman than 'Get Well Quick, FINK'?*"

*"Mr. Binns! Do we have any sick
'get-well' cards?"*

"How many are coming to the party?"

After June 1st, doctors joining the Health Service from overseas will not only have to prove they know the Queen's English, but, says a *Daily Telegraph* report, coyly, tests will be framed to discover if they understand colloquialisms such as "tummy" and "spend a penny"

(*Extract from "Medicina Senza Lagrime"—Fratelli Mafiosi, Dopolavoro Sicilia.*)

Scalpel, swab, scissors, lights . . . phrase-book

by J. E. HINDER

Lesson III. Up at the Surgery.

Doctor Lampeggia: Ah, Mrs Brown, I have not seen you here last week!

Mrs Brown: *No, Doctor, I was poorly!*★ (★Popular antique British jest. Not comprehendable to the Europeans.)

Doctor: Ho-ho-ho! So, how's your belly off for spots, me old dutch!★ ★(Not serious medical querying but Popular antique etc., as above.)

Mrs Brown: *How you are the joker, Doctor! No, I have come here again with my leg. I was believing her to be all tiggetty-boo but, dammit, she's up the creek again proper!*

Doctor: Truly? Shed then, old girl, the galosh . . . Hmmmm! She is, veritably, a bit of a mess. How your family has suffered from the legs and the plates of meat!

Mrs Brown: *Yes, chronic, Doc! By Bacchus, our ma was up Perkin Park with them more often than not and when she wasn't there she was down the Infirmary.*

Doctor: By the by, how is your daughter, Mrs? Not, let us hopefully conjecture, in the pudding-club once more?

Mrs Brown: *Not Pygmalion likely! Upon the pill with regularity is that one! But her tubes play her up something cruel this damp weather.*

Doctor: Unfortunate one, she! And son Elvis?

Mrs Brown: *Right as the rain except for a touch of the gastric.*

Doctor: Good is! Replace, for favour, the galosh. Now, I'm just giving you some pink pills and a spot of the old liniment, which should take the trick like a dose of salts!

Mrs Brown: *Good-oh, Doc!*

Doctor: Oh, and how goes the old hubby that is on the books of my mate, Doctor Bruttascosa?

Mrs Brown: *On the club down with his bronchial up in bed, Doctor! But still . . . making a nuisance of himself . . . eh . . . Doc. . . . a nuisance? Nudge-nudge!*

Doctor: Guard well, then, Mrs, that you do not cop out, discerning tardily that you are in the way and e'er one could cry "Peter Robinson" finding a visitation from the stork with a little bundle!

Mrs Brown: *I should cocoa, Doc! It was not yesterday I was born!*

Doctor: Good is! Here is your prescriptive note. Forget not to take two of the pills before retiring.

Mrs Brown: *But, Doctor, ho-ho-ho, I shall not be sixty for many years yet!*★

★(Popular antique British etc., etc., as above.)

Doctor: You are the merry wag, Mrs Brown! Oh, regard the hour! I must make speed, as I have the permission of the Chief Boilerman of Perkin Park Hospital to remove a pair of tonsils this evening!★

★(Modern British politics joke. Not comprehendable by Europeans.)

"Have you seen your own doctor?"

A Touch of 'Flu by GRAHAM

"I'd be grateful if you'd stave it off until Dickson gets back from his."

"It's a mild type apparently."

"*They sent a boy round with it.*"

"*They say hot whisky and water works wonders.*"

"*I think I feel strong enough to watch a little television this evening.*"

Doctor Patel's Diary

Immigrant doctors who speak correct English complain that they find it hard to understand quaint English dialects used by patients. MILES KINGTON presents one case history

March

Sometimes I wonder why I ever came to this backward country from India. I am not discouraged in my mission to bring health and enlightenment to the British—it is merely that they seem so slow to shake off their old superstitions and barbaric ways. I often think back to my Indian college days where all was so neat and clinical, and then I think with a sigh of my patients. There was a man this morning. He said his leg was playing him up.

"I beg your pardon," I said.

"Me leg. It's playing me up."

"Could you be a little more precise?"

"Ah. Well, to be dead honest, doc, it's giving me merry hell."

I asked him to explain it in correct English.

"I've got pains in my leg."

I chided him for not having said so before and asked him if it was the first time.

"No, doc. I always get it when there's rain about."

They are like children. How can a civilised man believe that his arthritis is caused by the weather? I do not think he actually believes in a rain god—they are all godless savages—but I would not be surprised. I explained to him patiently, in correct English, the cause of his ailment.

"Thanks," he said. "I'll tell you another thing causes it. A north wind. Think there's anything in these copper bracelets they talk about?"

April

Mrs. Wardrop has been three times this month. She is trying to shake off 'flu, or, in correct English, influenza. But she insists there is a bug going round. She is the fifteenth person who insists that there is a bug going round. Twelve said they don't feel well in themselves. Another five claimed to be under the weather. (The weather again!) None of them can describe their symptoms without a great deal of urging and prodding. They have no conception of scientific medicine. Or of English, come to that.

May

Of course, the big trouble is that they are used to their own quack doctors, as they call them. These are British GPs who work on the old tribal methods, believing that a patient can be cured by faith. I had a new patient yesterday, a Mrs. Partington, and my goodness she is one of the worst, I am telling you.

"I got a right dickey throat, doc," she said.

After ten minutes patient conversation, I have managed to elicit a description of her symptoms from her, without any of these unintelligible dialect words like dickey, lousy, rough, gammy, rotten or orrible. (I once had a New Zealand patient who claimed to be "real crook". I had sent for the police before he explained what it meant.) I diagnosed her ailment as pharyngitis, and prescribed a new drug which I find very efficacious.

"That can't be right," she said. "Dr. McIntyre always gave me red and yellow pills. They did the trick."

"Madam," I said. "I am telling you that this is the cure for your discomfiture."

"I wouldn't know about that," she said, "but Dr. McIntyre gave me red and yellow pills. They worked a treat."

A curse on all these primitive Dr. McIntyres and their primitive juju.

June

I wrote earlier that my patients are godless savages. I was wrong. Today a female patient claimed to be suffering under a curse. After twenty minutes careful interrogation it emerged that she thought of her menstruation as a curse! I think she wanted an incantation.

July

A curious man in my surgery on Monday. At first I thought he was subject to delirium but it turned out that that is how they speak in the region from which he comes, called Scotland. It is a fascinating dialect. I gathered he was suffering from pink eye, which is indeed a painful affliction, oh yes. But I could find nothing wrong with his eyes.

"Your eyes are quite all right," I said. "There is nothing wrong with you."

"Eyes? Whit ye're havering aboot, mon?" he said (The transcription is approximate.) "It's ma hand!"

He poked his little finger at me.

"Your little finger?" I said.

"Aye," he said. "Ma pinkie, ye ken."

I made a note in the essay I am preparing on British dialects: the Scots refer to the little finger as a pinkie. How he managed to get it stuck in a whisky bottle and dislocated it is a mystery which we never elucidated.

August

We doctors are not the only Indians attempting to convert the population of Britain. The missionaries have, as usual, got here first. Why is it that the spread of civilisation is spearheaded by the myths and creeds of the priests? Anyway, I was approached today by a Mrs. Firkin who is a firm devotee of our Indian beliefs.

"I am absolutely crazy about Yoga, Doctor," she said. "It is absolutely divine. You can't imagine what bliss it has brought me. I am a new woman. These super exercises have done me a power of good."

To cut a long recitation quite short, she had been carrying out some of the harmless ideas of our Indian gurus as if she really believed in them, and had sprained an ankle. I told her how to treat it and gave her a short warning.

"Do not imagine that you British have a monopoly of super-stition," I said. "If you wish to adopt Indian wisdom, come to a doctor first."

September

Today, for the first time, I met one of the most primitive of English tribesmen. I have made full notes elsewhere, but let me just say that he was a country-dweller, living on his own patch of land, tending his own flock of deer and goats. I have never seen such an unspoilt fellow even in England. His name was the Earl of Godalming. His dialect was almost completely bereft of meaning...

"Well, look, the trouble, don't you know, is that, as it were, I get this funny feeling, damned hard to describe, sort of, odd twinge, get me? That sort of thing."

I really must start writing a book. *My Life Among the Stone Age British? An Indian In Outer Europe?* In any case, I cannot continue much longer in this back-breaking effort to convert the natives. They are charming folk but quite impossible.

His trouble, by the way, was a simple case of gout, caused by the local fermented spirit.

"Sorry—only six persons allowed in the lift."

Licensed Hospital

For the first time ever, a London hospital has been granted a liquor licence. LARRY drinks to that

The Cure

Drunks should not be arrested but sent to a
drying-out centre, says a Government report.
ffolkes investigates.

"You're improving, Finnegan, that makes
twenty-five minutes without your elbow
moving."

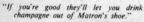

"If you're good they'll let you drink
champagne out of Matron's shoe."

"Dammit, Battersby, whose side are you on?"

"Doctor, come quickly! They're operating an illicit
still in the Brendan Behan Ward!"

"He says that he's absolutely cured and that we can
keep the rabbit."

110

The Avoidance of Stress and Worry BY M.D., F.R.C.P.

E VERY doctor in general practice knows the patient with waxy complexion, rapid pulse, tremulous limbs and thick speech; he knows too that there is nothing wrong with this man that a month in the Bahamas would not put right. He has been worrying; and if he can be persuaded to talk it will be found that he has allowed his imagination to inflate some trifle out of all proportion. His house has fallen through into a mining subsidence, perhaps, or he has been unexpectedly sacked and is having to take his children away from their public schools. The result is what doctors call among themselves an "anxiety state", meaning that the patient is in a state of mental anxiety.

Prevention Better . . .

The condition need not be fatal. The cure is to remove the cause. The cause is worry. Ergo, stop worrying. Beyond this advice, plus a prescription for an old-fashioned bromide, there is not a lot that a doctor can do. It is up to *you* to prevent the condition from arising, and this may be done in several ways.

News

Resist addiction to the daily papers. 1976, like 1975, is bound to give rise to world events, and you should take care to concern yourself only with those that affect you. Begin by ruling out earthquakes. The odds against getting caught in one are heavy. The same is true of nuclear explosions. Reflect that all atomic weapons tested to date could have exploded without your direct knowledge; for your purposes, therefore, they may be said to exist only as ink-marks on newsprint. Turning to events nearer home, how many persons of your acquaintance have actually fallen from a fourth floor on to iron railings? Been gored by bulls? Bound and gagged by masked gunmen? Ignore these reports. You will not only keep your mind free of unnecessary anxieties but effect a great saving on your newsagent's bill. Tuck this away into a savings account, ready for the half-yearly tax demand.

Noise

With improved techniques, next year is likely to be noisier than ever, and physicians are agreed that the sound of jet aircraft, pneumatic drills, soda-machines, champion Sealhyams, trumpet solos and so on, entering the nervous system through the delicate mechanism of the ear, can cause drunkenness, axe-slaying and other manifestations of imbalance. To these will shortly be added the penetrating hum of earth satellites, the boom of interplanetary missiles, the searing roar of departing moonships.

Over a period, of course, nature will adjust; the ear will grow less sensitive, smaller, perhaps ultimately disappearing altogether; but 1976 may be over before this happens, and our problem is one of the moment. What is to be done about noise? Again, the answer is

After a full day, adopt a relaxed position.

simple. Don't listen.

Wax ear-plugs are sometimes helpful at first.

Radiation Sickness and So on

Health scares will still be about in the New Year. Asian influenza has on the whole been such a failure that something particularly malevolent is bound to follow it; paralysis caused by invisible fumes released from household plastics has been named as a possible, and may well add to the mental insecurity of a man already convinced that if he hasn't got lung cancer his bone structure is slowly crumbling as a result of having slept every night for forty years beside a luminous alarm clock. Close your mind to all this; if you can't, concentrate on one branch of suffering and let the rest go hang. Slipped discs will still be in, and may prove the very thing. Above all, try to wean yourself from the dangerous habit of reading every health article you pick up. You never know what you might pick up.

Useful Drugs

Should all these hints fail to comfort, there remains, luckily, a wide range of wonder drugs. The following are obtainable at all good chemists:

Condition	Drug
Stress caused by TV serials, party political broadcasts, etc.	Cathodrayolite
Fear of missed trains, buses.	Tempone
Anxiety about vegetable garden pests.	Agricone
Sense of impending annihilation by noiseless flash.	Whiskidrene
Suspicion of petty theft by domestics.	Domestophone
Depression following dismissal from employment.	Sackarene
Strain induced by reading school reports.	Scholastoplite
Fear of habit-forming drugs.	Pharmaceuphthalene

112

My Medical Article

By BASIL BOOTHROYD

MORE and more doctors, hiding behind their professional anonymity, are stealing into print in the large-circulation dailies, taking care to say nothing to make the reader afraid, embarrassed, or likely to change to another paper. A continuous stabbing pain in the chest? Indigestion. Splitting headaches day and night, beyond the reach of bathroom-cabinet analgesics? Change your glasses. Giddiness? Eat more fruit.

I warn editors, I'm a pushover for any paper to publish *my* medical article:

In my experience as a humble G.P. I repeatedly find the patient pitifully self-deluding. Take Mr. X, who last week entered my surgery complaining of a pain in his toe. "It is nothing but an in-growing nail, I am convinced, doctor," said he, and asked me to prescribe a little cotton-wool to push under it. A glance showed me that Mr. X was in an advanced state of *incurionis litotes*, and calling in my receptionist we had the leg off in a jiffy. Once more I had had an example of nature's warnings ignored. During the very same surgery Mrs. Y came hurrying in. Luckily I had hidden X's leg under a blanket. She felt, almost ashamed to bother me she said, but she had had difficulty in breathing during the night, and had been obliged to get up and take a cup of tea in the small hours. "It is a touch of bronchitis," she said. Fortunately I preferred to rely on my own diagnosis—Cattermole's Disease—and was able to arrange for the early removal of the gall-bladder. It is not generally realized that congestion in the respiratory system is seldom a simple matter, but if left unchecked can speedily affect the knees, stomach-muscles, colon, pelvic girdle, and ears. The same is true of banged funnybones.

Sometimes of course the patient knows what is the matter with him, though only subsconciously; this leads him to make a joking reference to the nature of his complaint. A Mr. W called on me complaining of pains in the back. His wife, he said, was convinced that they were due to watching the television in a draught. "But actually," he grinned, "I expect it's granular disintegration of the kidneys: there's a name for it, now . . . " I said "Exactly. Bright's Disease. Do you mind dialling 999 and we'll get an ambulance in no time."

Of the last dozen patients to summon me to their homes, eight thought they had feverish colds, two complained of lumbago, one felt dizzy after a fried-fish supper, and the other insisted that he had a boil coming on his neck. After my examinations I found I had four pneumonias, three anginas, one smallpox, two shingles, one leprosy and one Blagmire's Disease (softening of the shinbones) on my hands.

Do not ignore small pains and discomforts. They are nature's warning. A shrill pinging in the ears, if not caused by a nearby mosquito, may mean that the brain is working loose; a strangulated cæcum is often heralded by pains in the calves; malevolent crystals forming between the frontal and parietal bones of the skull signify the imminent onset of *flagitis* or Old Man's Dithers, but early symptoms are misleadingly mild, being no more than a drowsiness after meals. Remember that the human body is a highly complex machine, with a thousand and one things to go wrong. A state of over-all health in any individual system is so rare as to be almost freakish, and it should be remembered that in treating one ailment you may well be giving a fingerhold to another.

In conclusion, bear in mind that we doctors know very little. There are many hundreds of diseases that have not even been discovered yet. You probably have them all. Have you made your will?

I offer the first British serial rights of the above to any publication but *The Lancet*—which is using much the same sort of material already.

Doctor. "Ah, we must have you at my Nursing Home."
Patient. "But Doctor, you don't understand. I'm feeling *really* ill."

Dowager. "So you are commencing a practice here. You're rather young, aren't you?"

Young Medico. "Oh—er—well—I only expect to start on children first, you know."

THE POWER OF IMAGINATION

Street Arab (to Doctor, who has just been taking his temperature). "Ah, Sir! *That* done me a *lot* o' Good, Sir!"

PRECAUTIONARY MEASURES

Local Practitioner (as he goes through his day-book and ledger).
"Old Smith hasn't called me in lately about his indigestion. You'd better ask him to dinner."

The Mystery of Medicine

WE perceive that MR. MUNTZ has given notice of a motion requiring all medical practitioners to write their prescriptions in English, and to put plain English on their gallipots. If this proposal is adopted, the dignity of Medicine is gone, for on the principle of *omne ignotum pro magnifico*, people fancy that a prescription must do them a wonderful deal of good if they cannot understand the meaning of it. Who will have any faith in medicine when he knows the ingredients?

There is something mysterious in *Duæ pilulæ factæ cum pane*, but when we come to know that it means nothing more than "two bread pills", the senses revolt against the idea of deriving any benefit from taking them. Besides, when a medical man is in a hurry, and does not know exactly what to prescribe, he can always with safety scribble down *Aq.—Cochl.—pan.—Sen.—Mag.—Cort.*, and the apothecary, if he has any tact, will send in something harmless, with directions—at his own discretion—about the mode and period of taking it.

But if all prescriptions are to be in English, what on earth is a medical man to do when he wants to prescribe nothing at all, but a dose quite at the discretion of the chemist. We knew a facetious general practitioner who used to jot down *qoud—plac—mi—form—car*, which looked very well in abbreviated Latin, but which was in short—or rather in full—*quodcunque places, mi formose care*—(whatever you please, my pretty dear;) a prescription the chemist always understood to mean water with a dash of senna in it, to be taken at bedtime. We entreat MR. MUNTZ to pause before he strips medicine of that mystery which gives it half its importance in the eyes of the multitude. As to anglicising the gallipots we defy the best linguist on earth to translate into English those mystic syllables which are painted at random with a view to variety, and without the remotest attempt at meaning.   1845

"IN MEDIO TUTISSIMUS"

Country Practitioner (*about to go up to London on Business*). "I shan't be more than Ten Days at the furthest, Mr. Fawceps. You'll visit the Patients regularly, and take Care that none of 'em Slip through your Fingers—"

An Ideal Medical Board

(*A Dream of the Future*)

I WAS due to go in front of the local Medical Board next morning, and I was seeking distraction in the evening paper. Suddenly my eye was caught by the headlines announcing the transfer of recruiting arrangements from the Military to the Civil authorities. This promised to be interesting.

All at once the room grew misty, and when the atmosphere cleared again I found myself in the open street. Before me was a palatial building with the words "*Medical Board*" carved on a marble slab over the main entrance.

I entered, and was immediately confronted by a liveried janitor who bowed obsequiously.

"I have come to be medically examined," I explained.

"Yes, Sir," he replied. "Will you be good enough to wait one moment, Sir, while I settle with your taxi-driver, and then I will take you to the waiting-room, Sir."

"I have no taxi," I said. "I just walked."

An expression of concern passed across his face.

"Oh, you shouldn't have done that, Sir. The Authorities don't like it. There is a special fund for such expenses, you know, Sir. Will you please come this way, Sir?"

I followed him along the corridor, and was shown into a luxurious apartment overlooking a pleasant garden. The janitor placed an easy chair in position for me, handed me a copy of *Punch*, and brought me a glass of wine and some biscuits.

"Now, Sir, if you will give me your papers I will send them up to the Board."

I handed the packet to him, and he left the room.

A few minutes later a message-girl entered.

"Are you Mr. Smith?" she inquired.

I confessed that I was, upon which she handed me a sealed envelope. I opened it, and found a letter and a cheque for five pounds. The letter ran as follows:—

"SIR,—The above-named Medical Board regrets its inability to examine you to-day. As you are no doubt aware, it is contrary to its rule to examine more than three persons in one day, and an unusually difficult case, held over from yesterday, has upset all its arrangements.

"The Board would consider it a favour if you could make it convenient to call again to-morrow morning at the same time.

"The enclosed cheque is intended to compensate you for the unnecessary trouble to which you have been put.

"Your obedient Servants ————"

Medical Officer. "Sorry I must reject you on account of your teeth."

Would-be Recruit. "Man, ye're making a gran' mistake. I'm no wanting to bite the Germans, I'm wanting to shoot 'em."

Punctually at the time appointed I again entered the building, and was met by the same janitor.

"The Board is quite ready for you, Sir," he said. "Will you please ascend to the dressing-room, Sir?"

He committed me to the care of a lift-girl, who conveyed me to the second storey. Here I was handed over to a smart valet, who assisted me to undress in a comfortable little apartment replete with every convenience.

Having donned a warm dressing-gown, I was conducted to the Board Room, where I found a dozen of our greatest Specialists assembled. The President shook hands and greeted me effusively. Then I passed in turn from one Doctor to another, each making, with the utmost delicacy and consideration, a thorough examination of that part of my anatomy on which he was an acknowledged expert.

When this was over I was invited to retire to the dressing-room and resume my garments while the Board held a protracted consultation on my case, On returning to the Board Room, I was provided with a seat, and the President addressed me.

"Well, Mr. Smith, we can find nothing constitutionally wrong with you. But tell me, have you ever had any serious illness?"

I shook my head. I had always been abnormally healthy.

"Think carefully," he urged. "We don't want to pass you as fit if we can help it."

He seemed so anxious that I felt ashamed to disappoint him.

"Well," I replied, "the only thing I can call to mind is that, according to my mother, I had a severe teething rash when I was ten months old."

As I uttered these words the faces of all became suddenly grave.

"That is quite enough, Mr. Smith," said the President. "You are given total exemption. You should never have been brought here at all, but I am sure you will realise that in times of national emergency mistakes of this nature are bound to occur. If you will apply to the Cashier on your way out he will give you a draft for twenty pounds, to reimburse you in some small way for the loss of your valuable time. Good-bye!"

He held out his hand, but before I could grasp it a mist again enveloped me, from which I emerged upon the dreadful facts of life.

1917

Physician. "And would you like to be a doctor, Jack?"
Mother (*while Jack is still hesitating*). "No, no! The dear boy couldn't kill a fly!"

NEWSPAPER HEADINGS POPULARLY ILLUSTRATED

"Influenza microbe discovered at a London Hospital"

"RALLYING"

Doctor (sotto voce to his Colleague). "We must reduce the Fever and abate the Thirst!"
Patient (who had overheard). "If you'll redooce the Fever, Gen'lemen—I'll uld'take—to abate the Thirst myshelf!!"

124

Hay Fever

THAT is the twenty-seventh time to-day!
What is the use of Nobbs's Nasal Spray?
What use my aunt's "unfailing" recipes?
There *is* no anodyne for this disease—
Thirty, I think! Another hanky, please—
        A-tish-oo!

The world is gay; the bee bestrides the rose;
But I blaspheme and madly blow my nose.
For shame, O world! for shame, the heartless bee!
Your sweetest blooms are misery to me;
And as for that condemned acacia-tree—
        A-tish-oo!

Oh, could I roam, contented like the sheep,
In sunlit fields where, as it is, I weep;
Oh, to be fashioned like the lower classes,
Who simply revel in the longest grasses,
While I sit lachrymose with coloured glasses—
        A-tish-oo!

Fain would I spend my summers high in air;
At least there are no privet-hedges there.
But even then I have no doubt the smell
From slopes celestial of asphodel
Would fill the firmament and give me hell—
        A-tish-oo!

They tell me 'tis the man of intellect
The baneful seeds especially affect;
And I that sneeze one million times a year—
I ought to have a notable career,
Though, at the price, an earldom would be dear—
        A-tishoo!

Gladly, indeed, to some less gifted swain
Would I concede my fine but fatal brain,
Could I like him but sniff the jasmine spray
Or couch unmoved within a mile of hay,
And not explode in this exhausting way—
        A-tish-oo!

1917

MATERIA MEDICA

American Physician (to English Ditto). "Now in Vienna they're
first-rate at Diagnosis; but then, you see, they always make a point
of confirming it by a Post-Mortem!"

EPISODE IN HIGH LIFE

(From Our Jeames's Sketch-book.)

The Lady Kerosine de Colza. "I cannot tell you how pleased I am to meet You here, Dr. Blenkinsop, and especially to go down to Dinner with you."

Dr. Blenkinsop (an eminent Physician, much pleased). "You flatter me, I'm sure, Lady Kerosine!"
Lady Kerosine. "Oh no! It's so nice to sit by Somebody who can tell you what to Eat, Drink, and Avoid, you know!"

FASHIONABLE ENTERTAINMENTS FOR THE WEEK

"Going to the Throat and Ear Ball, Lady Mary?"

"No—we are engaged to the Incurable Idiots."

"Then perhaps I may meet you at the Epileptic Dance on Saturday?"

"Oh, yes—we are sure to be there. The Epileptic Stewards are so delightful!"

BETTER
THAN EXPECTED

Medical science has advanced so far, says RICHARD GORDON, that it is now actually capable of combating illness

CRICKET was really invented by Dr. W. G. Grace in 1870, and medicine by Dr. Gerhard Domagk in 1933. Before these two imaginative practitioners, both pursuits were lively, rough-and-tumble, hit-and-miss affairs, quite unlike their precise, predictable, and generally unexciting forms today.

There had admittedly been such earlier innovations as asepsis, which exorcised from the operating theatre the surgeon's picturesque frock-coat, needles threaded with sutures stuck through the lapels like a fisherman's flies. And anaesthesia, which apart from the benefit of oblivion divorced speed from surgery, the wristy operator previously advancing on his victim over the sawdust-filled blood bucket like an impatient duellist. Dr. Domagk introduced the first antibiotic, enabling the physician in most complaints to do *something*, where formerly he could generally do nothing effective at all.

How lucky we are today, when antibiotics are not only freely prescribed by doctors for previously lethal complaints, but for many on which they have no effect whatever. If they are already producing more dangerous problems than they solve, and may one day be killing more people than they cure, we can meanwhile splash happily in the antibiotic flood tide before it turns on a shore littered with the nasty wrecks of former clinical enigmas.

The pre-antibiotic doctor of course did more than simply sit at the bedside, like the one in Luke Fildes's famous and touching picture—as James Bridie put it, "Scratching his beard and wondering what the devil is the matter with the sick child he is expected to cure." He did a great deal to convince himself, and even on occasion his patient, that suffering was being relieved and life preserved. As his therapy was ineffective, it had to be spectacular. The patient's blood was extracted under as painful and unpleasant circumstances as possible, preferably by leeches. All medicines had to taste foul. External applications like mustard plasters showed success by bringing away a fairly substantial area of skin. As today's middle-aged will remember, a particularly vicious attack fell upon the bowels. The textbook treatment of almost any condition started by advising "a good purge," doubtless because only purgatives could be relied upon to work, thus establishing from the start a valuable confidence in the skill of the practitioner.

It is not grasped by the public how surgeons are as susceptible to changes in fashion quite as much as couturiers and film producers.

In the 'twenties, the Charleston and long cigarette-holders were accompanied by a trend to remove as many internal organs as possible compatible with the continuance of life. Sir Arbuthnot Lane was inclined almost to eviscerate his patients as a cure for such disorders as headaches. The 'thirties saw padded shoulders, Hollywood musicals, and a change in surgical view. Organs were then tacked into place with stout catgut, firmer than ever. The floating kidney was discovered, careering about inside like a drunken sailor, to be disciplined by ingenious incarceration behind the ribs.

Then came the 'forties, the War and headscarves, and septic foci. Everyone was convinced that pockets of infection hidden in the body (some so cleverly as to be totally invisible except to the expert eye of the operator) caused a variety of complaints from migraine to rheumatism. They were searched for as religiously as medieval anatomists sought the site of the soul, and eradicated like a madman's devils. Then the profession forgot about them, I fancy through the horrific diversions of the coming National Health Service. In the mini-skirted 'sixties the rage was surgical transplants, a fashion mercifully restricted in application, which will doubtless become another barbarous memory with the introduction of neat, implantable machines to do the job of faulty vital organs.

How lucky are the young today! They have a vast selection of drugs for their preservation, amusement, or degeneration, a highly organised and skilful "free" Health Service at their command, and even a public attitude to abortion which in the days before antibiotics would have been almost as murderous to the mother as to the child. Had it not been for the earnest nutritionalists of earlier this century, our present youthful generation would not be swinging at all, except on swings. The age of sexual maturity has been falling steadily at the rate of four months a decade until it is now about thirteen, largely because our children are better and more sensibly fed. The skill and devotion of bio-chemists in gas-lit laboratories changed one of our leading social problems. It is no longer rickets at four months, but pregnancy at fourteen.

Our hospitals may admittedly look much the same as a hundred years ago, but how refreshingly the atmosphere has changed inside them. Patients are no longer treated as clamant paupers, to be

briskly stripped of their clothes, possessions, and personalities by the ward sister. In the style of the age, the inmates are hypersensitive about their rights and have even an Association to protect them. They sue for enormous damages at a whiff of malpractice. Such mishaps as the removal of the wrong limb, or even the performance of the wrong operation altogether, could pass largely unnoticed in times when the surgeon, like the Pope, was accepted as infallible and made his pronouncements in incomprehensible Latin.

How much more comfortable it has become to be ill! "At the foot of every bed," predicted Aldous Huxley, "confronting its moribund occupant, was a television box. Television was left on, a running tap, from morning till night." Of all the chilling visions in *Brave New World* this alone has come true. Oh, lucky us! Why, now we can even watch our favourite programmes right until death do us part.

Grannie. "And wit's the matter wi' me right leg, Doctor?"
Doctor. "Oh, just old age, Mrs. MacDougall."
Grannie. "Hoots, man; ye're haverin'. The left leg's hale and soond, and they're *baith* the same age."

131

CAUTION

Patient. "And if I have gas I shan't feel nothing?"
Dentist. "Nothing whatever."
Patient. "And I shan't know what you be doin'?"
Dentist. "You won't know anything."
Patient. "Well, just wait a minute till I've counted my money!"

A CONSULTATION

Patient. "Doctor, my Memory has recently become shockingly bad."
Doctor. "Indeed? In these Cases, Sir, it is my invariable Rule to ask for my Fee in advance."

HIGH LIFE IN THE COUNTRY

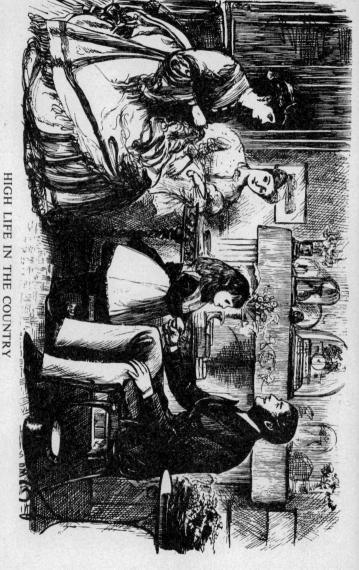

Doctor. "I am pleased to say, Mrs. Fitzbrowne, that I shall be able to Vaccinate your Baby from a very Healthy Child of your Neighbour, Mrs. Jones—"

Mrs. Fitzbrowne. "Oh Dear, Doctor! I could not permit that. We do not care to be mixed up with the Joneses in any way."

134

A DOMESTIC TRAGEDY

Our Doctor. "I'm sorry to say, old man, it's appendicitis, and you must have the operation next week."

Sister Dorothy. "It's *very* cowardly *and* wicked to have the operation; why can't you bear it like I do? I've had appendicitis for years, I am sure. You'll be away from work for weeks, and think of the trouble and anxiety you'll cause us all."

Aunt Fanny. "Are you *sure* your doctor is competent to undertake the operation? Some doctors are *dreadfully* careless. One, who operated on a poor friend of mine, accidentally sewed up his hat and gloves in his patient."

Sister-in-law Sydney. "So you're going into a nursing home for the job? Hope you'll like it. You'll probably catch something else or die of starvation, like a man I heard of who got forgotten. Well, goodbye and good luck to the carving!"

Friend Robert. "I thought I'd just look in to see if you'd paid up all your insurances, made your will and got everything in order. I thought, too, I could save your widow trouble if ——"

Our Doctor. "Sorry, old man, a mistake in my diagnosis; you've not got appendicitis; you're all right. Get up, it's your wife's pastry; *I've just had some!*"

FORCE OF HABIT—(A TABLEAU FOR FAMILY PEOPLE ONLY)

Adolphus, George, and Louisa, are Playing in Kensington Gardens—to them the Family Doctor unexpectedly. A. and G. and L. go through the expressive pantomime of Putting out their Tongues as a matter of course.

O Death Where is Thy Sting-a-ling-a-ling

Vincent Mulchrone laughs all the way to the grave

THE first bribe I ever took as a reporter was half-a-crown. I was seventeen, and he was dead.

"Would you like to have a look at him?" the widow asked. Office instructions on the point were explicit. I looked.

The other women in the little West Riding kitchen gathered round as the handkerchief was lifted from his face for the umpteenth time.

He was my first corpse, and for the first time I heard what was to become a familiar litany—"Ee, doesn't he look lovely? . . . Better in death than in life, Sarah Jane . . . Doesn't he look like himself?"

I was backing out when the widow reached under the tea caddy on the mantelpiece and handed me the half-dollar. I composed my pimply features and explained that there was no fee. This, I said, was journalism.

But I must take it. *He* had left it for me. But he didn't know me. She knew that.

"Before he died," she explained, "he said, 'When I've gone, they'll be sending somebody round from t'Observer. Tell him to have a pint wi'me—and tell him to get t'bloody thing right.'"

By chance I came across his funeral tea. They were burying him with ham at the Co-op Hall. There was tea—great, steaming, practically untouched urns of it.

The Co-op was run by Primmers, but the janitor wasn't one, and winked an eye at the bottles smuggled in from the pub over the road. The therapy stopped short of a knees-up. But I've been to worse *parties*.

The feast was splendid. The widow, who conceded that I'd "got it right," explained that, as well as the insurance, she'd had him in a club. There are still scores of burial clubs listed with the Registrar of Friendly Societies, survivors of hundreds started in Lancashire early in the nineteenth century to avoid a pauper's grave and provide a bit of a do for the mourners.

The Friendly Funeral Society, founded 1815, offered the relatives a benefit of 48s.—and 2s. more "provided they have beer to the amount of 4s. where the collecting box is." The link between pubs and funerals is an old one.

A funeral used to be an occasion, sometimes grand, sometimes boozy, generally a great display but always, one might almost say, full of life. Corpses were always "beautiful", funerals always "lovely". Now it's twenty-five minutes at the crematorium (and a "fine" if the clergyman runs over time), a peek at the flowers on the way to the gate, and a cup of tea in the parlour.

Where we used to see them off with ham, now we do it with high speed gas. An ad. in the funeral trade press says, "High Speed Gas— chosen by over ninety-six per cent of Britain's crematoria." Where, one wonders, are the leisurely four per cent?

A man used to lie in his own church and be buried in his own churchyard. Now the body goes to a "chapel of rest" and its disposal becomes an embarrassing sanitary exercise set to Muzak.

Well, say the undertakers—3,500 of them run a £60 million-a-year industry—we offer chapels of rest because vicars can't afford to heat churches for just a few hours.

And because so many families are out of touch with the church the undertakers frequently hire a clergyman most mourners have never seen before and may never see again.

He will officiate for as little as a guinea. The only briefing he needs if the crematorium, too, is strange, is on the location of the button that will send old Fred sliding stage Right to the Gas Board's special pride.

The great majority of those who go—600,000 of us every year—no longer believe in that damnation which gave point to the fear of death. Why, then, the antiseptic ritual, the bottling of emotions, the conspiracy to pretend that death has not occurred and nobody is grieving?

Death, it seems, has superseded sex as the last taboo. In his book *Death, Grief and Mourning*, Geoffrey Gorer convincingly concluded . . . "death and mourning are treated with much the same prudery as sexual impulses were a century ago."

Certainly our squeamishness about death and the mechanics of disposing of the body is utterly irrational. We try to deny the facts of death and loss. The Victorian convention of giving up social activities for a time has almost gone. Unlike mourners in Europe, we have stopped wearing full mourning.

"Must keep busy," we say. "Think of the future. Life must go on." Occasionally the dead themselves anticipate this and insist on paying for a last round for the boys from the coffin.

An old Yorkshireman recently left instructions for his cortège to stop outside the George and Dragon, where he had left a fiver for the purpose. Said his son, "As he was a happy man who looked on this as his last joke, we played it out."

Andre Simon, the wine writer, ordered champagne for his memorial service. A Cheshire publisher arranged his own funeral stage party. His son said, "Father had a wonderful sense of humour."

Old men, you see, with a glint in their eye, and memories of funerals as they used to be. The publisher expressly directed that there should be no wailing women at his funeral.

A Halifax widow, certainly no boozer, felt so strongly about the misery of modern funerals that she forbade mourners to come near hers. Instead, said her Will, ". . . after my coffin has been removed I want my friends and neighbours to drink three bottles of champagne, provided by me."

Not that drink is essential to give a funeral a bit of a lift, a touch of style. One of the handsomest funerals of this year was that of an old farmer who insisted on being buried in his own garden alongside the graves of his dogs.

In Caerphilly there's a bricklayer who makes them his hobby. He got hooked on his mother-in-law's funeral fourteen years ago and now goes whenever he can, whether he knew the corpse or not.

"Sometimes he comes home a bit depressed," says his wife. "But nothing, not even cricket on the telly, his other big love, keeps him here if there's a funeral on."

The amateur mourner himself says, "I don't like fussy funerals. I can't stand all the crying. I like the ones in the Order of Buffaloes best. There's always some good, strong singing, and people looking happy."

When that grand old engineer, William Foden, departed at the age of ninety-five a few years back, he rode out on Pride of Edwin, a steam traction engine he built himself in 1916. Marching ahead of the coffin, blaring in blazing scarlet, went the Foden Motor Works championship brass band. Now *there's* a way to go.

You don't get the *racy* funerals of old any more. It's ten years now since Johnny "Scarface" Carter, Sid the Con, Nick the Ape and Freddy the Fly were at a funeral together down Camberwell way.

The deceased was a motor trader whose £6,000 Cadillac crashed in flames near Tower Bridge, and so many of the lads turned out that the cortège stretched for a mile. The best wreath, by general consent, was a four-foot billiard table with six legs of red carnations, a green moss surface, and a set of ivory balls and a cue. Lovely funeral.

They can be happy affairs. I was at Pandit Nehru's funeral along with about half a million others, and that was quite a gay scene, with vendors selling chupattis and pop in the crowd. They watched his body pass and smiled fondly because they do not make our mistake of equating the corpse with the life that was in it. There was no hush. How could there be, when everybody wanted to say goodbye?

The English scoff at the Irish wake, not appreciating that it has nothing to do with dogma or superstition, and very little (apart from a prayer or two) with the corpse, but a great deal to do with sustaining and cheering the living.

I survived one in West Cork earlier this year. Then his friends, as is the pleasant custom, dug the old sailor's grave, but not too deep, for they soon struck another coffin. He barely got below ground, and in the hush a voice said, "Jaysus, he hasn't got six inches of freeboard." Everybody smiled. Why wouldn't they? They loved him.

Our funerals have become mean, miserable, embarrassing affairs with, at crematoria, as much style as a production line. Dammit, the Chinese hire men to bang gongs and carry crazy floats. We go with a hum of tyres and a hiss of gas. Taped music, an optional extra, is used for solace the way the big jets use it just before landing.

When I go, give me a Basin Street funeral band, Belgian black horses with plumes, a stop at the tap room of The Hermit, and lots of ham. It won't bother me, mate. But it might just take that miserable look off *your* face.

When you've Got to Go

A few grave digs from HEATH

It would be nice if everybody had a good cry as I'm sure I will be missed. The thought of the crowds (after all I am the Rudolf Valentino of the cartoon world) sobbing around my grave quite brings a lump to my throat.

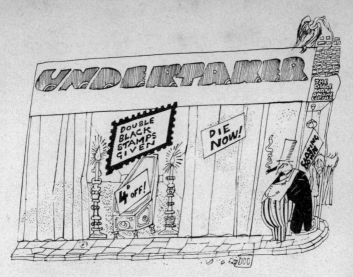

The Supermart Owner. Trussed up and frozen in an airtight plastic bag the Supermarket Owner can die as he lived. There is four pence off this funeral as it is considered a loss leader by "Multi Undertakers" who specialise in dealing with the little man on the corner.

Suggestions for David Frost's funeral (a long way away David, we hope, super!) Guests will be invited to speak (pausing only for commercials) on the subject of how wonderful it is to be invited etc. The word death will not be mentioned instead: "We'll be back in a trice" will be repeated ad nauseam. A tape recorder and mike will be buried along with a clipboard just in case. His ten writers will also be put to death and buried with him. (It's in their contracts.)

143

The oldest student in the world even when dead, refused to do as everyone else, and had to be beaten into the coffin with a heavy rock LP. Luckily the burial was free, as a grant covered all expenses. He was buried with ceremonial pumps or bumpers, and prayers were said to the martyrs St. Oz and St. It and children's crusader Richard Neville.

The film producers last end (or fade out) a special screen on the grave will show continuous screenings of "The Sound of Musak" and "Uneasy Rider", the remarks that killed him. Mourners will Q in the rain (ice cream, nuts, etc, are on sale in the crypt) and prayers are asked to be said to almighty box office.